Ears to Hear

EARS
TO
HEAR

AN INTRODUCTION TO THE FIRST FIVE BOOKS OF THE BIBLE

Winifred M. Green

 the bible reading fellowship

Text copyright © 1994 Winifred M. Green

Published by
The Bible Reading Fellowship
Peter's Way
Sandy Lane West
Oxford
OX4 5HG
ISBN 0 7459 2829 3
Albatross Books Pty Ltd
PO Box 320
Sutherland
NSW 2232
Australia
ISBN 0 7324 0897 0

First edition 1994

A catalogue record for this book is available
from the British Library

Printed and bound in Great Britain
by Cox & Wyman Ltd, Reading

Contents

Foreword
by John Barton
Vice-Master of St Cross College, Oxford

People sometimes tell me that they have decided to read through the whole Bible, and ask if I have any advice. Until now my advice was has always been *not* to 'begin at the beginning'. For though Genesis appeals to most Christians, in Exodus the going is harder, and by the end of Leviticus most readers have given up.

But Winifred Green's book shows that my advice 'Don't begin with the Pentateuch' is needlessly fainthearted. Drawing on her long experience in adult education she is able to guide the reader through even the darkest passages in Genesis–Deuteronomy. What is more, her explanations do not explain away the difficulties that readers have always found in these books. On the contrary, she shows exactly why the difficulties arise. In the process the reader is introduced to the fruits of modern biblical scholarship, and comes to understand how these often puzzling books came to be written. Instead of being flat, two-dimensional objects they become living utterances of real men and women, who lived in many different settings and times in the life of ancient Israel, and who bore witness to their faith in God by telling and retelling the stories which made them the people they were. As we see the original settings of the stories in sharper focus, we do not find that they are more distant from our own concerns; the more we learn about their original meaning, the more we find that they can still speak to us of the God to whom the Bible witnesses, the same yesterday, today and for ever.

I know of no other book that introduces the ordinary Christian reader to the Pentateuch in this way, and hope it will be widely read by everyone who has ever felt they should get down to reading the Bible, but did not know where to start. The beginning is, after all, the right place to begin!

John Barton

Preface

'He that hath ears to hear, let him hear.'

Abraham and Moses both heard the voice of God, and through their obedience changed the course of world history. Accounts of their struggles and achievements are found in the first five books of the Bible; Christians know these as the books of Moses, Jews as the Torah, which is the word of God, his will for his people.

As these books were completed some two thousand years ago they are not easy reading for us today. Convinced however that the word spoken then is still valid and that we neglect it at our peril, I have attempted to write an introduction that will enable us to 'read, mark, learn, and inwardly digest', so that in our turn we may hear and obey.

My thanks are due to Dr John Barton, Vice-Master of St Cross College, Oxford, who has kept me from straying from the insights of modern scholarship and has given me much help and encouragement, and to Daphne Martin-Hurst, without whose generosity and criticisms my book could never have been written. I am obviously indebted to many translators and commentators. I should also like to thank James Barnett who by inviting me to provide a course on the Pentateuch for Readers in the Diocese of Oxford, first led me to begin the project. We all share the hope that this book will be of value not only as an introduction for those who are preparing for a more detailed study, but also to many who are struggling to understand and follow the way of Jesus. Jesus was a Jew, and these are the Scriptures in which he was brought up. He heard the Torah read Sabbath by Sabbath, and in the Synagogue school he learnt it by heart. By the time he was twelve years old he was questioning the Rabbis in the temple about its meaning. By the time he began his public ministry he had so made its teaching his own that he spoke 'with authority and not as the scribes.' His whole life and teaching was based on obedience to the will of God as revealed in these Scriptures so that we may see him as their embodiment—the Word made flesh.

List of illustrations

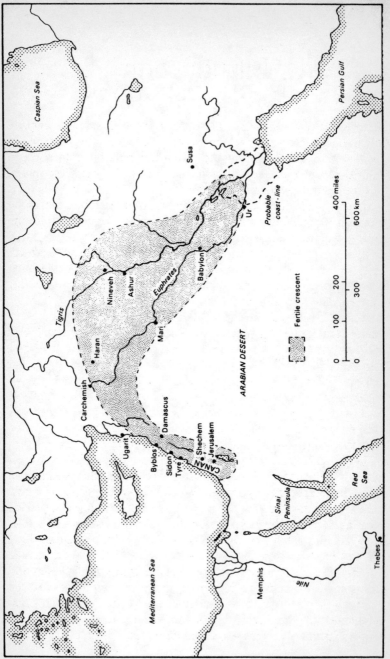

1. Map to show the Fertile Crescent

—— CHAPTER I ——

Introduction

History records more than one exodus, more than one escape of downtrodden peoples from oppression. Such an exodus occurred in 1968 when about four thousand of the Hambukushu tribe escaped from Angola. What makes the exodus of the children of Israel so special that we call it *the* exodus?

In many ways the exodus of the Hambukushu resembles that of the Israelites. Both groups were insignificant when compared with the great power from which they escaped. Neither event hit the headlines, or their Egyptian equivalent. Each tribe had suffered forced labour; each had been pursued by soldiers. They had both struggled through water to freedom, and had arrived on the farther shore destitute, frightened, hungry and exhausted.

Because Israel is so theologically significant we tend to overlook its unimportance at the time of the exodus. A study of a map of the Middle East will soon correct this. Measure, for example, the distance between the river Jordan and the Great (or Mediterranean) Sea, and compare it with that between Thebes and Babylon along the trade route through Damascus. Sometimes the area we know as the Holy Land was a troublesome outpost of the Egyptian kingdoms, sometimes it was the battle-ground between the great powers of Egypt and Mesopotamia. Only for a bare three hundred years did it have an independent existence (see chart, page 10).

The physical needs of the Hambukushu people in 1968 were met fairly speedily by the Botswana Christian Council and the International Red Cross. A retired missionary priest, Ronald Wynne, who happened to be visiting the area, stayed with them for over seven years, sharing their life, learning their language and listening to the tales they told. They had no written records, nor indeed, any written language. They had however many resemblances to the Israelites. Like the Israelites the Hambukushu believed in one creator God who made the sun and moon, and who controlled their crops. In the arid part of Africa which had been their homeland they had lived in scattered groups, but had come together periodically for worship. This included sacrifice and a ritual recitation of past heroes; a condition of sharing in the ritual was

11

being in love and charity with each other. It was not long before Ronald Wynne was able to talk to the Hambukushu about the Israelites whose position had been very like their own, and who had learnt from their own deliverance that God had been with them in their struggles—he was not only their creator, but also their redeemer.

Humanly speaking the situation of the Israelites had been even more hopeless than that of the Hambukushu. No outside agency came to supply their needs. Everything depended on the wisdom and skill of Moses, to whom the people complained bitterly that they had left the fleshpots of Egypt only to perish in the wilderness. Was it simply Moses' knowledge of the desert which had taught him where to strike the rock in order to release a hidden spring? Was it coincidence that they crossed the path of migrating quails, or found the sweet manna? Moses convinced the people that it was due to the providence of God. By all accounts Moses was a man of outstanding ability, but he was more. We are told he was a man 'who speaks with God as a man speaks with a friend' (Exodus 33:11), and we can well believe it. It is from his interpretation of events that the faith of Judaism and of Christianity has arisen. A recital of the Exodus is still repeated every year by Jews at their Passover celebrations, and Christian celebrations at Easter are redolent with it. For Christians see in the death and resurrection of Jesus the same pattern of God's saving power that Moses saw. The events recited in the annual rituals of Passover and Easter are passed on to succeeding generations, being preserved by the corporate memory of the community in the same way as were the rituals and traditions of both the Hambukushu and the Israelites, before ever they were written down.

MOSES AS INTERPRETER

The exodus would not have been memorable had it not been for Moses; he led the Israelites from service of the Pharaoh not merely to freedom, but to service of God. The books which record the tradition of the exodus and of all the events and teaching which together welded a depressed group of frightened slaves into the people of God are together called the Books of Moses. They are the first five books of our Bible. In spite of their diversity, they form a unity, which we are apt to overlook when we use their more familiar sub-titles—Genesis, Exodus, Leviticus, Numbers and Deuteronomy. These difficult names derive from the Greek translation which was used by the Jews in Asia · Minor to whom Paul preached. They are sometimes collectively called the Pentateuch, which means simply, the Five Books. In the Gospels they are known as an entity, 'Moses'. In the parable of the rich man and Lazarus, Abraham said, 'If they do not hear Moses and the prophets, neither will they be convinced if one should rise from the dead.' On the road to Emmaus we read of the risen Jesus, that 'Beginning with Moses and all of the prophets, he interpreted to them in all the Scriptures the things concerning himself' (Luke 16:31; 24:27). We find the same thought in John, 'If you believed Moses, you would believe me, for he wrote of me' (John 5:46).

Moses' faith is the inspiration behind the Pentateuch; he is not its literal author. At the lowest level, how could he have written about his own death? Even the earliest chapters of Genesis bear signs of having been written some time after the events they record. The phrases, 'The Canaanite was then in the land' (Genesis 12:6; 13:7), and, 'before any king reigned over the Israelites' are obvious editorial asides from a later writer; so also is the phrase, 'to this day' (Genesis 19:38; 35:20). Probably not until the Israelites were fully settled in the Promised Land was the first account of the exodus written down (see Figure 2). After David's wars had brought peace to the land and Solomon was reigning in glory over a vast empire, there were wealthy professional classes with both leisure and skill in the art of writing (1 Kings 4:3). This was roughly as far as after the exodus as we today are after the Spanish Armada. Those who wrote the Pentateuch were not contemporary to the events they describe, and it is not a record which can be guaranteed historically accurate in every detail; indeed there are repetitions and discrepancies. What we have is not the precise historical method we have come to expect in our computer age; it is *faith-history*. Past events were interpreted by people with a living faith, and retold to minister to that faith.

During the time of oral transmission many traditions developed into sagas, and local variations occurred. We are accustomed to reading the Bible in snippets; a more continuous reading reveals duplications. Compare, for example, Genesis 17:16–19 with 18:10–15, or Genesis 27:27–29 with 28:1–4. As we read further we shall discover other duplications and discrepancies, evidence that the books have been compiled from different sources. The Pentateuch did not take its final form until some time after the exile, in the sixth century BC. All that can be said for certain is that it was translated into Greek before the year 200BC, when the Hebrew version would already have been in circulation for some time. There was a Samaritan version which is older than this. Was 'the book of the law' which Ezra brought back from the Jews in Babylon to

13

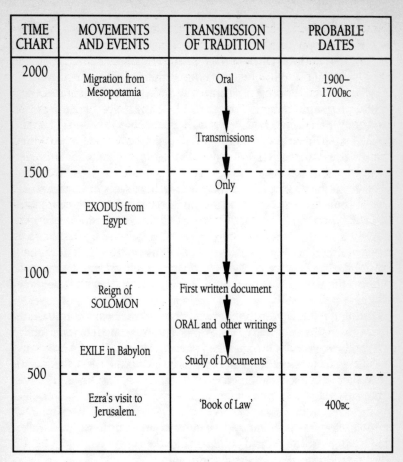

TIME CHART	MOVEMENTS AND EVENTS	TRANSMISSION OF TRADITION	PROBABLE DATES
2000	Migration from Mesopotamia	Oral	1900–1700BC
		Transmissions	
1500	EXODUS from Egypt	Only	
1000	Reign of SOLOMON	First written document	
		ORAL and other writings	
	EXILE in Babylon	Study of Documents	
500	Ezra's visit to Jerusalem.	'Book of Law'	400BC

2. Chart to show relative times of oral and written transmissions of tradition

read to the people who had returned to Jerusalem the whole of the Pentateuch? (This reading is recorded in the eighth chapter of Nehemiah.) If it was, it must have been completed by about 400BC.

THE BOOK OF THE LAW

'The Book of the Law' is the name by which the Pentateuch is known in the Gospel according to Saint Matthew, rather than 'Moses' (Matthew 22:40). The English word 'law' however, is an inadequate translation of the Hebrew word 'Torah', which is the name used by Jews today for the

14

Pentateuch. Torah has overtones which are missing from modern English conceptions of law. Originally it meant instruction about the will of God, and was often applied to specific incidents; for example, David asked for Torah about attacking the Philistines (2 Samuel 5:22–23). Much later, the prophet Haggai sent to the priests for Torah about a matter or ritual cleanness (Haggai 2:11). Sometimes Torah might be written; we read that 'Joshua wrote all these laws in a book' (Joshua 24:26). In the Pentateuch there are indeed what we in the West would recognize as law; the Ten Commandments spring to mind. There is also much that is akin to our case-law, for example, 'If you meet your enemy's ox or ass going astray, you shall bring it back to him' (Exodus 22:4). There are instructions for keeping festivals, and for treating skin diseases; there are even instructions for removing mildew from the walls of a house. Then there are general exhortations which seem to us more like sign-posts than laws. 'You shall be holy as I am holy', and, 'You shall love your neighbour as yourself.' There are also stories, told not for entertainment alone, but for their teaching about the way in which God acts.

During the five hundred years after the exile in Babylon the idea of Torah gradually deepened until it could be applied to the whole of the written Scripture about the beginnings of the people of God. Some indication of its full meaning for Jews can be discovered by meditating on the last part of Psalm 19, verses 7 to the end, or on the long acrostic composed in praise of the Torah, Psalm 119. Judgments, statutes, precepts, are some of the words used to describe Torah. These are not surprising, but others are; faithfulness, loving-kindness, testimonies and word are all present. The opening verse of one section gives the idea of guidance,

Thy word is a lamp to my feet and a light to my path.
Psalm 119:105

To call the Torah the 'word of God' is not to imply that every word in it is directly inspired by God, still less that it was written at his dictation. A word is the expression of a thought, and 'Who has known the mind of the Lord?' (Romans 11:34 from Isaiah 40:13–14). Only the language of poetry can begin to suggest the majesty of the One who 'laid the foundation of the earth', and 'makes the clouds his chariot, and rides upon the wings of the wind'.

A poem or even a single line of poetry needs more than one man's lifetime in which to yield its meaning; not only what the poet intended, but the reverberations of what he wrote, which come echoing from the circumstances of other times are full of meaning for us now.

Alan Ecclestone

So the word of God heard in ages long past by a people living in a distant land has even deeper richness for us. The circumstances and style in which it was originally understood may be strange to our ears, but the word is the word of the eternal and unchanging God. It comes to us across the ages, yet speaks to our present situation. Like the meaning of a line of poetry the full meaning of the word comes to us only as we live with it. This is not a matter of keeping laws, however important these may be, but of living in the awareness of the redeeming love of God. Even the direct commands of the Decalogue are prefaced by a reminder of that steadfast love; they are a response to it, not a blueprint for keeping the right side of a tyrannical, heartless power. 'I am the Lord, your God, who has brought you out of the land of Egypt, out of the house of bondage.' Only in this personal relationship can the word be heard and understood. Only 'he that hath ears' can hear. Pre-eminently the Old Testament prophets listened and understood. So it is that the Torah does not stand alone; it needs the insights of the prophets. The Law and the Prophets are still read in conjunction with one another in synagogues today as they were in the time of Jesus. By studying them we shall not only understand better the Jews of today, but also the mind of Jesus, whose whole life was based on obedience to the Torah, even to his death.

SUGGESTIONS FOR DISCUSSION

1. What do we mean when we say after a Bible reading, 'This is the word of the Lord'?
2. The Bible says God spoke to Abraham. What does this mean in today's terms?
3. Listen to any chance talk, say in a bus or on a visit, and notice how seldom people really listen. How can we listen to God?

NOTE ON VERSIONS AND TRANSLATIONS

Abbreviations in common use

AV	Authorized Version, or King James' Bible	1611
RV	Revised Version	1885
RSV	Revised Standard Version, in USA first	1952
NEB	New English Bible, approved by main denominations	1970
CB	The Common Bible, an English version of the RSV approved by the major Churches	1973
JB	The Jerusalem Bible, a Roman Catholic revision	1966
GNB	Good News Bible — Evangelical	1976
NIV	New International Version	1979
NJB	New Jerusalem Bible	1985
REB	Revised English Bible	1989

One of the difficulties of translating any ancient literature is that many of the words have fallen out of use, so their meaning can only be guessed at from their context. In some versions there are notes, either in the margin or at the end of the page, reading, 'Heb: obscure'. Other notes may indicate a reason for changing a word or a phrase from one given in an earlier translation. For example, the AV and RV both report that the Queen of Sheba said to Solomon, 'Happy are thy men!' In the RSV this has been altered to, 'Happy are thy wives!' with the footnote, 'Gr, Syr:wives, Heb:men' (1 Kings 10:8). The significance of these abbreviations and of two others which sometimes appear may be summarized as follows:

Gr.   The translation of the Hebrew Scriptures into Greek commonly called the Septuagint, completed before 200BC, and in use in the Mediterranean area during the time of Paul. This is the reason why some of the quotations in his letters do not exactly match our version of the Old Testament.

Syr.   A translation into Syriac, a dialect of Aramaic in use in Mesopotamia.

Tg.   Targums or Teachings. After Hebrew had ceased to be a spoken language the verses read in the synagogue were repeated in Aramaic. Later these were written down, not as translations— the Hebrew text is considered too sacred for that—but as explanations, e.g. where the Heb. says that Adam and Eve 'heard the Lord' in the garden, the Targums say they 'heard the voice of the word of the Lord God'. Targums are not reliable texts, but they throw light on the way a passage was understood.

Vg.   The Vulgate, the translation into Latin made by Jerome in the fourth century AD. After translating the New Testament and the Psalms, Jerome went to Bethlehem to study Hebrew from a rabbi. So the Vulgate, which had a great effect on Western Christendom, is not only the most scholarly of the early texts, it also reflects the understanding of fourth-century Judaism. Jerome's earlier translation of the Psalms had already become so popular that it remained in normal use for chanting, and it is this version, translated into English by Miles Coverdale in 1535, that is used in the 1662 Book of Common Prayer. (However much loved this may be, it is not a reliable translation.)

The Hebrew text

A community of Jews in Tiberias, known as the Massorites, during the sixth–tenth centuries AD produced a transcription of the ancient Hebrew with a system of tiny symbols between the consonants to indicate the correct vowel sounds, as Hebrew had long since ceased to be a spoken language (see page 14). This transcription, known as the Massoretic Text, (MT for short), has been the standard text since the tenth century, and all extant copies of Hebrew Scriptures have been made from successive copies from it.

Great care is taken in copying, which is governed by elaborate rules to ensure accuracy. In spite of its late date, the general accuracy of the MT has been supported by comparison with a copy of Isaiah found amongst the Dead Sea Scrolls which were hidden before AD135, and also with a copy of the Samaritan Pentateuch. (The separation between Jew and Samaritan seems to have been complete by the beginning of the second century BC.)

English Versions

Although parts of the Bible, notably the Gospels and the Psalms, had been translated into Anglo-Saxon, it was not until the fourteenth century that the whole Bible was translated, under the inspiration of John Wycliffe. This was suppressed by the Pope, as was also that made in 1525–29 by Tyndale. In 1535 Miles Coverdale dedicated his translation to Henry VIII. Knowledge of Greek and Hebrew increased, so did the number of translations, until in 1604 a conference arranged for a new translation using the latest scholarship. This was completed in 1611 and 'authorized to be read in churches'. This, the AV or King James' Bible, was used for many centuries, until it was revised in 1885, making use both of recent scholarship and of more modern language. Scholarship continued to make new discoveries, and the turmoil of two world wars made a translation into current language a matter of urgency. The RSV was produced first in the USA, followed by the NEB in this country. These are all produced by the Protestant Churches; Roman Catholics and Orthodox have approved the use of the Common Bible, an edition of the RSV using English spelling and including the Apocrypha, some books of which are recognized as scriptural by the Roman and Eastern Churches.

The New Jerusalem Bible is a revision of the Roman Catholic translation of 1966, 'making use of the advances of scholarship over two decades to provide a more accurate text and further assistance for understanding it.'

CHAPTER 2

Becoming the people of the book

Passages for study are given in the text

From an historical point of view alone the Jews are a remarkable people. In the book of Exodus we read of Hivites, Jebusites, Perizzites, of Hittites, Ammonites and Moabites—tribes and empires which have long since ceased to exist. Of the twelve tribes of Israel only Judah had survived by the time the Pentateuch was completed. (The name Jew is an anglicized form of Judah.) That even Judah had survived is as remarkable as its continued survival during the next two thousand years. All the international importance acquired in the reign of Solomon had been lost, first to the Assyrian Empire and then to the Babylonian. The Babylonians destroyed not only the holy temple built by Solomon, but also Jerusalem itself, carrying into exile almost all the population. In its turn the Babylonian Empire fell, conquered by Persia, and some Jews went back to the ruins of Jerusalem. Greeks conquered Persia, and Roman power succeeded Greek. The Romans destroyed what had been rebuilt after many hardships by the few exiles returning, and since AD70 until a few years ago the Jews had no homeland, no central meeting place, no independent government. The Jews have ever since been scattered in small communities throughout the world, often suffering violent persecution. Amazingly, not only have they survived and retained their identity, but they have influenced the whole course of history. The secret of their survival is their reverence for the Torah.

To appreciate how a group of helpless refugees from Egypt developed into the 'people of the book' it is necessary to make a rapid survey of their history. This will help us also to understand the different points of view that are found in the Torah, since the total period of its formation covers some eight hundred years.

SETTLEMENT IN THE PROMISED LAND

After the Exodus there were 'forty years' in the wilderness, and it was a new generation that entered Canaan. As their numbers had increased

20

so had their separation into tribes. No longer may we think of them as a unified crowd advancing victoriously under one banner. The book of Joshua gives this impression, but it probably refers to one tribe only, as the book of Judges tells a very different story. According to the latter, the various tribes settled in different parts of the land, and never completely overcame the original inhabitants (Judges 1:19–20, 27–29). Whereas Joshua has been written to show the power of God to help those who trusted and obeyed, Judges is written from the complementary truth that failure to obey leads to disaster. The pattern is stated in Judges 2:11–18, and is shown in greater detail in 3:7–9. It is repeated with successive judges—Ehud, Deborah, Gideon and Jephthah. Figure 3 makes clear the recurrent cycle.

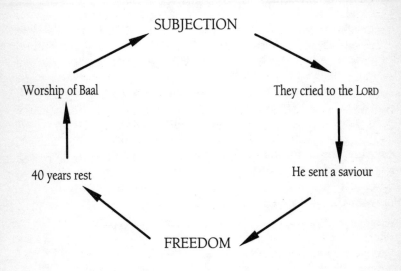

3. Diagram to show cycle of Judges

That the people should repeatedly resort to Baal-worship is hardly surprising when one remembers that they were adopting a completely new way of life. When they settled down to agriculture like the Canaanites, they naturally adopted all the rites and ceremonies connected with it. For Baal was the God of fertility. Tablets unearthed at Ras Shamra, an ancient Ugarit city near Tyre, have revealed a local variant of the myth of the struggle between the seasons—here between autumn fertility and summer drought. The

21

personification of destruction, Mot, overcomes Baal, the storm-god, who dies. Anath, Baal's sister-consort discovers him after a long and difficult search, and by her act of love, restores him to life. By re-enacting this mythological drama, the Baal-worshippers believed that his divine power would again be released, bringing rain to re-vivify the soil. Here is an extract from a prayer to Baal from the Ras Shamra tablets:

In a dream, O Kindly One, God of Mercy,
In a vision, Creator of Creatures,
The heavens rained oil,
The dry valleys flowed with honey;
So I know that triumphant Baal lives,
That the Prince, Lord of earth, is alive!

It was not easy for an unlettered peasant to realize how far this worship was from that of the Lord who had brought them out of the land of Egypt, so the worship of Baal and that of the Lord existed side by side, as the story of Micah shows (Judges 17).

The much embroidered saga of Samson indicates a new enemy, the Philistines, who were invading from the sea. The Philistines were not completely restricted to the coastal plain until the end of David's reign. The effect of their invasion was two-fold—it drove Israelite and Canaanite closer together (so increasing the worship of Baal), and it was responsible for the demand for a king. Kingship introduced a new concept, that of nationhood, and was later to give rise to conflict between church and state.

THE ESTABLISHMENT OF A MONARCHY

Saul was mainly concerned with fighting the Philistines. David's reign was also one of constant fighting, but by the end of it the country was at peace. David tried to unite the tribes by building a new centre of government on neutral ground, Jerusalem, which he had captured from the Jebusites. His shrewdest move was to make Jerusalem the most important centre for the worship of the Lord, by bringing to it the ark of the covenant. (This had had no proper home since its capture by the Philistines.) David was a notable musician, and according to the Chronicler, he organized the musicians into guilds (1 Chronicles 35). His contribution to the worship of Judah is remembered by the dedication to him of the book of Psalms, although it is not possible to discover how many of them he actually composed. David achieved

4. Sketch of god of storms, mounted on a bull

so much for Judah as a religious community that his weaknesses were soon forgotten.

Solomon consolidated what David had begun. His kingdom became a vast empire, by treaty rather than by conquest. An enormous central staff was needed for its management, and Solomon built up a magnificent court. He fulfilled David's dreams of a permanent building for the ark. This was another innovation, and later prophets saw that the temple had become more important than the Lord for whose worship it had been built (Jeremiah 7, 8–16). Solomon ruled as an oriental despot. His grandeur and his grandiose building schemes depended on forced labour, and on unprecedented tribute from the people of grain and oil (1 Kings 5:13–16; 9:15–24). The numbers in chapter 5 are doubtless unreliable, but the burden of forced labour clearly lay behind Jeroboam's request for alleviation (1 Kings 11:27, 28, 40; 12). Rehoboam's refusal of the request led to the separation of the bulk of the tribes from Judah. From this time there were two kingdoms.

THE TWO KINGDOMS

Jeroboam's rebellion had been supported by the prophet Ahijah, and the centres he chose for worship, Dan and Bethel, were both holy places associated with the Patriarchs. In setting up golden bulls his motives may have been entirely innocent, however misguided. Among Syrian relics there is a model of a bull acting as a throne for the god of storms; many people think that Jeroboam intended the bull to be no more than the throne of the invisible Lord; was not the ark in Jerusalem a similar symbol?

Bulls, however, were too reminiscent of Baal-worship to be anything but a temptation! The judgment of later generations places them at the core of Israel's downfall. This is the verdict of the writers of the Books of Kings. (These books are not intended to be a complete history; for this the authors refer the reader to the lost chronicles of the kings.) When the death of an Israelite king is mentioned an identical comment is made: 'He did that which was evil in the sight of the Lord; he did not depart from the sins of Jeroboam, son of Nebat, which made Israel to sin' (1 Kings 10:11, 22, 52). Kings of Israel are judged, differently from those of Judah, being compared to their father David. See for example, 2 Kings 15:11–14.

The unity of the tribe of Judah under a settled dynasty was one reason for its longer survival; there were repeated rebellions in the north as

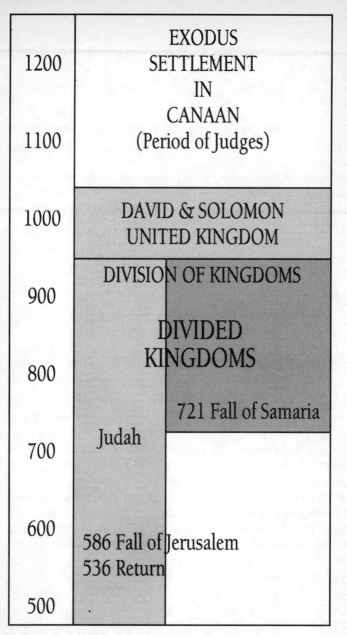

1200	EXODUS SETTLEMENT IN CANAAN (Period of Judges)
1100	
1000	DAVID & SOLOMON UNITED KINGDOM
900	DIVISION OF KINGDOMS
	DIVIDED KINGDOMS
800	
	721 Fall of Samaria
700	Judah
600	586 Fall of Jerusalem
	536 Return
500	

5. Time chart—from exodus to exile

can be seen by those who care to work out for themselves the pattern of kings. Here is a very brief summary:

	JUDAH		ISRAEL	
	PROPHETS	KINGS	KINGS	PROPHETS
900		Rehoboam	Jeroboam I	
		⋮	Omri c. 876 Ahab c. 869–852 Jehu c. 842–815	Elijah Elisha
800		DAVIDIC		
	ISAIAH MICAH c. 740–700	DYNASTY	Jeroboam II	AMOS HOSEA
		⋮	END	
700		⋮		
600		↓		
	EZEKIEL c. 597–570 Zephaniah JEREMIAH	Fall of Jerusalem		
500	c. 626–587 II ISAIAH c. 540 Haggi c. 520	**EXILE** Return		

6. Time chart—the divided kingdoms

Other reasons for Judah's survival stem from its position off the main trade route between Egypt and Mesopotamia. The northern kingdom was much more open to foreign influence, and received more of the benefits of trade. During this period of the divided kingdoms, the oracles of the prophets began to be written down.

When Israel was passing through a period of affluence Amos saw that her prosperity was founded on injustice and was therefore doomed to failure. Her women lay on ivory couches with silken cushions, drinking wine by the bowlful, while the poor were trampled in the dust (Amos 2:6–8; 6:1–7). Hosea, almost his contemporary, saw the impending doom as a direct result of the worship of Baal which he describes as harlotry (Hosea 2: esp. vv. 5, 8, 13). He poured scorn on the bulls erected by Jeroboam, and recalled the people to the Lord who had brought them out of the land of Egypt.

When Israel was a child, I loved him,
and out of Egypt I called my son …
My people are bent on turning away from me…
How can I give you up, O Ephraim,
How can I hand you over, O Israel?

Hosea 11

The prophets' pleading went unheeded; political expediency took precedence over repentance, and successive kings tried to keep the Assyrian threat at bay by increasing the amount of tribute they paid. Their struggle was in vain, and in 721BC Samaria was captured by the Assyrians, the northern kingdom of Israel was conquered and its population carried away to be lost for ever as the chosen people. Possibly a few escaped to the southern kingdom, there to work with religious leaders for the survival of the holy community.

After the fall of Israel when the Assyrians having captured some cities of Judah had come to the very walls of Jerusalem, Hezekiah, a devout follower of the Lord, turned to the prophet Isaiah for help. The dramatic story of the reprieve of the southern kingdom is told in Isaiah, chapters 36 and 37, as well as in the Book of Kings. Isaiah advised against going to Egypt for help, for:

The Egyptians are men, not God,
and their horses are flesh, not spirit.

Isaiah 31:13

Judah's salvation lay in returning to 'the Holy One of Israel':

In returning and rest you shall be saved.
In quietness and in trust shall be your strength.

Isaiah 30:15

Isaiah looked for the rebuilding of Jerusalem on the foundation of a faithful remnant (Isaiah 10:20, 21), and he saw it as coming through the dynasty of David, which had been such an important factor in Judah's survival, and in the maintenance of faith in the Lord. Here is the origin of the idea of a kingly Messiah.

Afer the death of Hezekiah, Isaiah's prophecies were disregarded by the court. During the fifty-five years of the reign of the next king,

Manasseh, not only was the worship of Baal restored, but Assyrian ways of worship were introduced. There is a devastating list of enormities in 2 Kings 21, possibly exaggerated, but certainly with a basis of truth. The followers of the Lord were not popular, but they were not inactive. The Levites, perhaps joined by others from the north, continued their teaching and preaching in the areas around Jerusalem. There were also those unknown scribes who wrote and hid the Law book which was discovered when opportunity for reform came with the new reign, and the temple was cleansed. The newly-revealed Law book was read with great solemnity to all the people, who joined in a new covenant ceremony (2 Kings 22–23). It seemed that the religious community had been reborn. The drastic reforms which Josiah introduced as a result of its discovery, described in 2 Kings 21, almost exactly match those in the twelfth chapter of Deuteronomy, and it is likely that this chapter formed at least part of the book of the covenant found in 621BC. We shall consider Deuteronomy in a later chapter, noticing here only two points, first that Josiah made Jerusalem the one place where sacrifice could be offered, and second, that the book discovered in the temple was no new law, but was based on old traditions. While the prophet Zephaniah regarded the world crisis as the judgment of the Lord, and the conquest of Israel by Assyria as the work of his hand (Zephaniah 1:4–18), Jeremiah saw further, that God's will was not only to destroy and overthrow, but to build and replant. Josiah's reforms had come too late. Both Jeremiah and Ezekiel lived through the troubled time which followed and which culminated in the fall of Jerusalem in 586BC and the carrying away to Babylon of the cream of the population. There had been however, a sufficient return to the Mosaic faith for Jeremiah to prophesy a new covenant (Jeremiah 34:31–34), and for Ezekiel to draw up plans for the rebuilding of the temple.

THE RETURN

Fifty years after the exile a return was possible, and even encouraged by the Persians, under whose domination the whole of the Middle East had now fallen. Few Jews of the new generation that had grown up in exile were prepared to face the journey to a poverty-stricken corner of the Persian Empire in order to rebuild a ruined city. For those who did return, life was hard, and first Nehemiah and then Ezra went back from Mesopotamia with the support of their rulers, to help their brethren in Jerusalem. The diaries of these two officials are in the books of Ezra and

Nehemiah—one book in the Hebrew Scriptures—but they are not in chronological order. The reforms which Ezra and Nehemiah carried out formed the basis of Judaism, with a solemn renewal of the covenant following the impressive reading of the Law book which Ezra brought with him (Nehemiah 8). This is the book which may possibly have been the complete Torah.

BETWEEN THE TESTAMENTS

This is where the Old Testament history ends, but it is far from the end of Judaism. A second result of the exile, apart from the collating and editing of the Scriptures, was the dispersion of Jews to many centres of commerce around the Mediterranean region, taking with them, of course, their Scriptures. It was in one of the largest of these colonies, Alexandria, that the Torah was first translated into Greek, probably in the reign of Ptolemy II (285–223BC). Tradition says that Ptolemy encouraged this translation as a step towards the Greek vision of one world, united under one culture. This had been the glorious ideal of Alexander the Great, who in his triumphant march eastwards had established his empire before he died in 323BC.

Like minority groups everywhere, the Jews of the Dispersion met together frequently to strengthen their common ties and to maintain their identity. Every bit of their heritage was remembered and studied. Sabbath by Sabbath they met together for worship and for the solemn reading of the Torah and the exposition which followed it. Other writings were also translated into Greek and eventually were included in the Septuagint, the Scriptures used by the early Church. The Scriptures were always available, even when the temple was far away, and synagogues and schools were established for their study. The shift from temple to Torah began to gather momentum.

Greek culture, however, had its attractions. Beautiful Greek cities were built in Palestine, and young people especially felt a surge of release in the Greek ideal of physical beauty. A gymnasium was erected even in Jerusalem. Opposition there was, but this was only a rumble until Antiochus IV decided to put a stop to it forever by wiping out the Jewish religion altogether. He forbade circumcision and the obser-vance of the Sabbath. He desecrated the temple, and burned books of the Law wherever they could be found. The story of the sparking of open rebellion is found in the first book of Maccabees. Notice that Mattathias' challenge was not about the temple, but was to 'everyone who is zealous for *the Law* and who supports the Covenant' (1 Maccabees 2:27).

In the face of great opposition the rebellion which Mattathias began and which was carried on by his sons (usually called 'The Maccabees') was successful. For a short time Judah together with most of the northern territory was free from foreign domination. But as always in any power struggle, the original vision was lost sight of in the struggle for power itself. Even the Hasmoneans, religious leaders who had supported the rebellion, quarrelled among themselves for the High Priesthood. Eventually the situation became so confused that the Romans, who had replaced the Greeks as the dominant foreign power, stepped in to take control. Antipater, an Edomite, was one of the few men who had kept their heads in more ways than one, and the Romans appointed his son Herod as king. Sporadic unrest continued until the Romans destroyed the Temple in AD70. Sacrifice was now impossible. There was one further attempt to regain freedom in 135, but this ended in disaster. Meanwhile a devout Pharisee, Johannan ben Zakkai, escaping from Jerusalem, had established a school in Jamnia for the study of the Scriptures for which many Jews had given their

7. Some key dates in post-exile history

538BC	Edict of Cyrus of Persia permitted return
520–515	Rebuilding of Temple inspired by Haggai
c. 500	Prophecy of Malachi
Between 458 and 398	Ezra and Nehemiah visit Jerusalem— Rebuilding walls, reading Law Book reforms
323	Alexander the Great conquered Syria and Palestine

Egyptian control of Palestine under the Ptolemies

285	Ptolemy II, who encouraged translation of Torah into Greek
198	Syria takes control from Egypt
176	Antiochus IV (Epiphanes) tried to obliterate Judaism
168	Maccabean revolt
63	Roman occupation
47BC	Herod the Great appointed king under Rome

lives, and which now became the basis of worship. Israel as a nation had ceased to exist, sacrifice was ended, and the Jews were at last a religious community. They were now 'The people of the book'. The Book of Exodus records their election, the covenant and its laws which bind them, and their religious rites.

NOTE ON THE CANON

The Pentateuch is but one part of the Hebrew Scriptures. Its teaching is derived from and coloured by the whole experience of the Jews, which therefore has a vital part in its interpretation. So too, have the many books which were written from that experience. We cannot evaluate the Pentateuch apart from the whole Jewish Scriptures. At first it was the popularity of the different books which determined their value. Only after AD93, many years after Nero's persecution of Christians was the final selection made of those writings which were considered author-itative and known as the 'Canon' of Holy Scripture. This is as follows:

1. The Torah
The five books of Moses, or the five fifths of the Law, known by their opening words.

2. The Prophets
Former prophets: Joshua; Judges; four books of Kings
Latter prophets: Isaiah; Jeremiah; Ezekiel
The Twelve: Hosea, Joel, Amos, Obadiah, Jonah, Micah, Nahum, Habakkuk, Zephaniah, Haggai, Zechariah, Malachi.

3. The Writings
Psalms; Job; Proverbs; The Festal Scrolls (Ruth, Song of Songs, Ecclesiastes, Lamentations, Esther); Daniel; Ezra–Nehemiah; 1–2 Chronicles.

The Hebrew Scriptures differ from English Bibles in two ways—in the order of the books, and in the way in which books which we are apt to regard as 'history' are classified. This is because Christian Bibles stem from the Septuagint, the Greek translation which was made before the Canon was fixed and used originally in the Dispersion, and so by the early Christians. The Jews, in fixing which books should be regarded as Holy Scripture rejected all those which had been written in Greek, for example, the Wisdom of Solomon. The books which had been in the Greek Bible but not the Hebrew were eventually separated in English Bibles to form the Apocrypha.

SUGGESTION FOR DISCUSSION

Are there events or patterns in Jewish history which have their parallels in the difficulties which confront us today (e.g. the relationship between Church and State)?

CHAPTER 3

In the Beginning

Passages for study: Genesis 1–2; Isaiah 40, 45

HOW DID THE WORLD BEGIN?

The Torah opens with a firm declaration of faith. 'In the beginning God created the heaven and the earth.' The Jews were alone in the belief in one God, until first Christians, and then Muslims arose to share it. The Canaanites had their fertility gods, Babylonians and Assyrians worshipped sun, moon and stars, and Greeks and Romans had a family of gods. One of the Pharaohs, Amenotep IV, in the fourteenth century BC had tried to introduce a kind of monotheism in which the sun's disc symbolized the supreme deity; his reformation was short-lived. Aristotle's 'Prime Mover', known only to an intellectual élite, was too cerebral to call forth man's adoration. It was in Athens, Aristotle's own city, that Paul many years later is said to have found an altar dedicated to 'The Unknown God'. The Jewish belief that the Creator of the universe was 'their' God, active in the affairs of mankind and leader of his people, has sustained them during unspeakable persecutions and pogroms. Readers may be familiar with the words found on the walls of a Polish concentration camp:

> *I believe in the sun even though it does not shine;*
> *I believe in love even though I do not feel it;*
> *I believe in God even though I cannot see him.*

Faith in one God is far removed from the myths of creation which were prevalent in the Near and Middle East. In most of these the earth goddess in some form or another, figures as the supreme power. She may be assisted by the winds or by the ocean. The latter is envisaged as surrounding the earth, and is often personified as a serpent. In some myths the ocean may be the home of the dragon who is in conflict with the benign powers who are working to bring order out of chaos. In others the miracle of life is seen as the hatching of an egg. One describes how the egg is crushed by the serpent, and from it spring all things that exist; another tells that the egg produces Eros, who then proceeds to create the world. The writers of the first three chapters of Genesis had far outgrown these early gropings after the mystery of existence. Some of the same words appear, e.g. chaos and serpent, but the concepts they represent are very different. In Genesis there is no conflict, no hatching from egg, no mother goddess; the whole creation depends on the will of the sole, supreme God.

THE BELIEF OF ISRAEL

Remembering the history of Israel, it is impossible to think that this was the faith of all the Israelites from the beginning! The Books of Judges and Kings in particular are full of the struggles of judges and prophets against the worship of false gods, whether these were the deities of earth and storm, or of sun, moon and stars and all the host of heaven (2 Kings 21:3). The writer of the first chapter of Genesis asserts in no uncertain terms that the sun, moon and stars, the earth and all that springs from it, may in no way be worshipped; they are all creatures of the One God. In the words of Psalm 8, they are 'the work of his fingers'. This concept of God is found in the unknown prophet of the exile, who is sometimes called the Second Isaiah, or Deutero-Isaiah, because his work is written on the same scrolls as those of the prophet Isaiah who lived in the reign of Hezekiah.

> *Lift up your eyes on high and see;*
> *who created these?*
> *He who brings out their host by number,*
> *calling them all by name;*
> *By the greatness of his might,*
> *and because he is strong in power not one is missing.*
>
> *Isaiah 44:26*

And again,

> *Thus says the Lord, the King of Israel*
> *and his redeemer, the Lord of Hosts;*
> *I am the first and I am the last;*
> *besides me there is no God.*
>
> *Isaiah 44:6*

God is not only creator, but redeemer and sustainer. Creation is not a completed, past event with the creation once set in motion and then allowed to continue on its own, like the watch found on the sea-shore, sometimes used in argument, still ticking although the maker has abandoned it long since. All matter is constantly in a state of flux; the creative power is continuously at work within it. This is the Jewish faith, that the power of God is immanent in creation, continually making and remaking. This dependence of all things on God which is an important tenet of both Jewish and Christian faith, is well illustrated in Psalm 104:

These all [i.e. both man and animals] look to thee
to give them their meat in due season.
When thou givest it to them, they gather it up;
when thou openest thy hand, they are filled with good things.

When thou hidest thy face, they are dismayed;
when thou takest away thy breath they die, and
return to their dust.

When thou sendeth forth thy Spirit they are created;
and thou renewest the face of the earth.

Psalm 104:27–30

Astronomers and biologists may hold different theories of the way in which the universe and the life on our planet developed; but Big Bang or continuous creation, natural selection or evolutionary leap, the method of God's action is irrelevant to the fundamental belief that all things depend on him.

Today we use the word 'created' very loosely, speaking of job-creation, and even of fashion creations, when concoctions might be a better word! In Hebrew the word create can be used only of God. Man cannot create; he manipulates. Even man's most creative works, poems and pictures, are but meditations on the works of God. God has only to speak the word and it is done. 'God said, Let there be light! and there was light.'

CREATION IN GENESIS

The first chapter of Genesis is like no form of literature known to us, hovering as it does between poetry and prose. It is unlike the Hebrew poetry we know from the Psalms and the Book of Job. It has sometimes been called a paean of praise, yet for all its majesty it has none of the personal involvement that is an essential part of praise. Besides recognizing the absoluteness and otherness of God, the chapter implies a plan and a purpose behind creation. This again matches the belief of Deutero-Isaiah, who, speaking for God about a return from exile says,

> I have spoken, I will bring it to pass;
> I have purposed, I will do it.

Isaiah 46:11

Although the first verse of the second chapter of Genesis tells us that 'the heaven and the earth were finished', verse five says there were not yet any plants or animals. What follows is another account of creation, with many points of difference from the first. It is worth writing out the differences in parallel columns, noting for example, the word used for the creator, the order and the manner of creation, the relationship between male and female, and the status and duty given to mankind. We will return to this later. There is one other point to notice in this chapter, viz., the seventh day.

The obvious place for the seventh day would seem to be at the end of the first chapter, yet it comes in the second, so the division into chapters seems to be badly done. In the original Hebrew text there are no divisions into chapters and verses; these were added later, simply for ease of reference. There is an example in the Gospels of the old way of reference, when Jesus quoted from 'the place concerning the Bush', where we should say, 'see Exodus 3' (Mark 12:26). Did those who made the chapter division make a mistake? Or were they perhaps making a point of doctrine? Creation continues; the 'rest of God' is still in the future. One is reminded of the saying of Jesus, 'The end is not yet.' Jews and Christians alike are people of hope, looking ahead to the perfection of all things.

Returning to the problem of two different accounts of creation, we have to ask, why? Obviously they cannot both be factually true, since they differ in so many ways. Nor can they be read as records of what actually happened on a particular day of a particular year. So what are the fundamental truths we can discover below the surface? Have we any clues about the origin of these accounts which will help us? We have seen how similar the concept of God is in the first chapter to that of Deutero-Isaiah who wrote during the exilic period, and it seems reasonable therefore to date this chapter about that time. The second account has a more primitive vision. The Lord moulds man from clay and breathes on his little figure; then he takes a piece from near man's heart and of it makes a help-meet. The simple story form also seems primitive, it is reminiscent of the sort of reply one would give to a young child's question, 'Who made the first man?' An early account certainly, but with no trace of mythological chaos or earth goddess. The sun, moon and stars are taken for granted, but the Lord is in charge, making mankind and commissioning them to look after the earth and the animals on it. Although the man was made first, the female shares his task; she is bone of his bone and flesh of his flesh. There is in effect very little difference from the male and female of the first account, where they are complementary parts of mankind. The main difference in the accounts lies in the understanding of God.

When early missionaries in South India were translating the Bible into Tamil, they found two words for God, and there was much discussion about which to use. One represents a friendly, loving spirit, so close to the villagers that they prepared clay horses for him to use when he rode round their homes to protect them at night. The other is the supreme Deity, the Ultimate Reality, far beyond the knowledge of the creatures he has brought into being. In Genesis, the friendly Lord of the second chapter has many of the characteristics of the homely Tamil 'devam', whereas in the first chapter the creator is like the remote, utterly transcendent God. It is the Jewish faith that both these aspects of the Godhead are true; God is beyond man's understanding, yet he cares tenderly for his creation.

The prophet of the exile who speaks of God as 'stretching out the heavens like a curtain', compares man to the drop that falls from a bucket when it is drawn up from the well, or to the dust on a pair of scales. Yet in the same magnificent chapter he writes,

He will lead his flock like a shepherd,
he will gather the lambs in his arms,
he will carry them in his bosom,
and gently lead them that are with young.

Isaiah 40:11

For all the greater understanding of the majesty of God gained through centuries of their experience of him, the Jews could not abandon the old story which too spoke of their experience. Neither can we, for all our knowledge of the universe. Its insights were too valuable to be discarded by the compilers of the Pentateuch, and they are still valid today. A new account was written of the creation, not to replace the old story, but to complement it.

Men and women can express their thoughts only in the words and idioms current in their own day. The early story belongs to a time when sun, moon and stars were unquestioned, and when it was natural to think of God in human terms. In Babylon however, the Jews had met a people who were renowned for their study of the heavens. The thought and language of both the first chapter of Genesis and Deutero-Isaiah show that this understanding of the vastness and order of the universe had been assimilated. Greek mathematics which could work out the diameter of the earth and postulate its global form, were as yet unknown in Babylon. Genesis pictures the earth as it appears from the centre of an enormous plain, with the sky seen as an overarching dome, the firmament, across which the heavenly bodies move in their appointed order. Digging below the plain, man finds water; water rains from on high. So there are waters under the earth and waters above the firmament. The story of the flood uses the same imagery, 'The fountains of the great deep burst forth, and the windows of heaven were opened' (Genesis 7:11; 8:2).

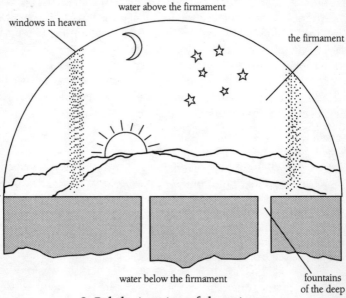

8. Babylonian view of the universe

The idea of primaeval chaos also belongs to Babylonian idiom. Their ancient creation myth involves a struggle between rival gods, Marduk and Diarmat, who dwell in chaos. There are slight references to the dragon of the deeps in the Psalms and in Isaiah, but these are probably no more than suggestive comparisons—the equivalent, perhaps, of giving a handsome youth today the title Adonis, the beautiful Lord of Greek mythology. There is nothing in the Torah to suggest an alien power of darkness; God is the sole reality. Darkness too, is his creation.

> *I am the Lord, and there is no other,*
> *beside me there is no god;...*
> *I form light and create darkness,*
> *I make weal and create woe,*
> *I am the Lord, who do all these things.*

Isaiah 45:5-7

This is the word of the prophet of the exile, in whose time, or after, the account of the creation in the first chapter of Genesis was probably written, i.e. in the late sixth or fifth century BC. The earlier story belongs to the first attempt to write a continuous history of God's choice of Israel from the very beginning, and it is usually dated about the time of Solomon. We know nothing about the writers, who may have been individuals or groups. Their interests and purposes may be gathered from their total contributions to the Pentateuch.

The two strands of writing found in Genesis are known to scholars as P and J respectively. There are two other strands of writing, E and D, which we will discuss when we meet them later in our study. The characteristics of J and P are as follows:

J uses a simple direct approach to God whom he knows as compassionate and friendly. He calls God by the personal name by which the Israelites came to know him as *their* God—YHWH—a word which has often from the thirteenth century onwards been mistakenly read as Jehovah, and which is in the RSV always written as The LORD. J probably came from the southern kingdom of Judah. His outlook is optimistic, and he was probably writing in a time of prosperity and expansion (this is why the reign of Solomon is suggested).

P (short for priestly) has a transcendent view of the majesty of God. He is interested in ritual, and in demonstrating by long genealogies that the Jews are the true inheritors of God's promises. He is not such a good story-teller as J! P's idea of God corresponds to that of the prophet Ezekiel, and, like Ezekiel, he is preparing his readers for a return to the Promised Land after a period of disaster.

Each source has its own contribution to make, and each uses ancient, traditional material. We know nothing about either of these sources, nor about those who collated .their work to form the complete Pentateuch. This they did without obscuring the special insights of each.

> All things are two-fold, one opposite the other,
> The Lord has made nothing incomplete.
> One confirms the good things of the other.
> And who can have enough of his glory?

> Ecclesiasticus 42:24–25

SUGGESTIONS FOR STUDY AND DISCUSSION

1. Find out some myths of creation in other faiths, e.g. Greek, Japanese, African.
2. Discuss the Genesis stories in the light of modern scientific knowledge. Do modern *theories* of creation undermine belief in a Creator God?

CHAPTER 4

Whence disharmony?

Passages for study: Genesis 3–11; Isaiah 1; Ezekiel 18

The Jews hold fast to the belief that 'The Lord is God and there is no other' (Isaiah 46:9). How then do they account for the suffering which has been the lot of mankind since 'Adam delved and Eve span'? The writers of the Torah see clearly that disobedience to the will of God brings disaster, a truth they felt had been demonstrated by the Babylonian conquest. Only after contact with Greek philosophy, some time after the Pentateuch had been completed, did the theoretical problem arise of the suffering of individuals for the sins of others. (It is discussed in the Book of Job, a late work.) During the exile, Ezekiel had voiced the responsibility of every individual for his own sin (Ezekiel 18). For J who was still thinking in terms of the whole community, it sufficed that suffering is the result of sin.

WHAT DO WE MEAN BY TRUE?

Before we consider the stories J collected to illustrate this truth, we would do well to remind ourselves that he is using ancient material. This is occasionally obvious, as in verses 10–14 in chapter 2 of Genesis. These verses seem to have no significance for us in the creation narrative, although they give us a glimpse of the limited world of the author, where water was of vital importance. There is another passage in chapter 5 where the genealogy of Cain fits very awkwardly into the story, prompting the irrelevant question, 'Where did Cain's wife come from?' There are other passages, more obvious to those who can read Hebrew than to those who read only in translation. We see here something of J's manner of working; he has woven a rich tapestry from ancient traditions that lie deep in the heart of human experience. So we need to read them, not as we read a telephone directory or an encyclopedia, looking for hard facts, but with the openness with which we read a poem or a great play, receptive to anything that corresponds with our personal experience. If these stories are not fact, are they then untrue?

I once discussed with a group of 11-year-olds what they understood by a true story. They knew that a biography of Madam Curie could be accepted as true, but not the tale of Doctor Dolittle; they hesitated over *Black Beauty*. They had all wept over it; they could not possibly say it was untrue. Then one of them suggested, 'Is it true to life?' and we were all happy! 'Is it a sort of parable?' came from another as we went on to look at the story of Adam and Eve. So we looked for what that was trying to tell us.

The proper theological term for a story of this kind is 'myth'. This is a word used loosely in common speech for something that is imagined. The imaginary element is present, but it is not important; it is simply a way of expressing a commonly felt experience.

The children all knew that the longer they looked at a temptation the more desirable it became, that disobedience is more fun if shared, and that it is always easy to blame the other person. O, yes, the story was true to life! They knew too, that the fear of being found out formed a barrier isolating them from those who loved them, and clouding their innocent enjoyment. This common human experience rings true regardless of the belief one has about the interpretation of the story that once upon a time a particular man and woman sinned and thereby caused all mankind to sin and suffer. Adam is not the name of a specific person, but means simply 'man'; Adam is Everyman, and Eve Every-woman. We all suffer from what the theologians call 'original sin'. It is sometimes known as the Fall, but, as William Temple pointed out, it is a 'fall upward', a step in the evolution of humanity. There must have been some point in the development of the human race, as there is in that of every human embryo, at which the individual becomes self-conscious, able to choose, and to act as a person. With self-consciousness comes the desire for personal gratification, wanting one's own way, which is, in effect, 'becoming as gods'. So 'Adam and Eve' in every generation eat of the fruit of the forbidden tree.

The serpent is one of God's creatures, but one that presents a challenge to man's pride. It has powers beyond man's ability, with its swift, uncanny movement, the sloughing of its skin, and above all, its power to kill with its deadly sting. Man's attitude to it has always been one of fear and awe. The serpent is reverenced in Hindu mythology, and it is the symbol of Aesklepios, the Greek god of healing. Because of this link with healing it figures on the badge of the Royal Army Medical Corps. There is a curious tale in the book of Numbers of the people being healed by looking at the bronze serpent which Moses set up—to cure them from the bite of scorpions! In Canaanite rites, which were a constant temptation to the Israelites during their settlement in Canaan, the serpent was a fertility symbol. God's curse on the serpent in the story of Adam and Eve means that the conflict between man and snake will continue, both on the obvious physical level, and also symbolically as the source of temptation. It is only in late Jewish thought that Satan appears as God's adversary, and still later is identified with the powers of evil. During a time of fierce persecution, the writer of the book of Revelation identified the dragon with 'that ancient serpent, who is called the devil and Satan, the deceiver of the whole world' (Revelation 12:9). Yet the seeds of this identification are present in the story of Adam and Eve. Good and evil seem to be inextricably intertwined in each of us!

The verses describing the perpetual conflict between man and serpent (Genesis 3:14–15) are sometimes taken allegorically to be a prophecy of the Messiah, but, whatever the compilers thought, this seems a long way from the thought of J. He was writing when the monarchy was flourishing, before any thought of a messiah was developed. Nevertheless J was aware of the hopelessness of the human situation; paradise and innocence had been lost; toil for man, pain for woman and uneasy relationship between them both were for ever the lot of mankind because of sin. It is not God who fails. He searched man out and talked to him in his shame. The 'sound of God' that Adam and Eve heard is the 'rustle of God's presence'—the same sound that David was told to listen for in the balsam trees (2 Samuel 6:24). When Adam and Eve first realized their nakedness they made themselves aprons of fig leaves; when they were turned out of the garden, it was God who provided them with coats of fur. The nearness of God, and his loving concern, are characteristic of J's writing.

WIDER RESULTS OF SIN

We find God's loving concern again in the otherwise terrible story of Cain and Abel. Even after Cain has been condemned to a life of wandering he is still under the protection of God. There are many difficulties in this story, and many things we would like to know but are not told. The differences in the way of life of Cain the farmer and of Abel the shepherd were so great that they did not even sacrifice on the same altar. We are not told why Cain's sacrifice was unacceptable. Whatever the original meaning of the story may have been, as J uses it here we are taken a stage further into the disaster of a divided humanity; not only is man outside paradise, he is at enmity with his brother man. When Cain refused to listen to God's warning and murdered Abel, he also alienated himself from the earth. Yet God was still present with him, asking, not as in the earlier story, 'Where art thou?' but, 'Where is your brother?'

At this point in the story J inserts a genealogy that has come to his notice. Its effect here is twofold; it gives the origin of music, of the cities, and of the use of metal which have so enriched the civilization of Solomon's vast empire, and it shows the great increase in evil which comes from man's pride in his achievements and his possessions. Lamech not only took on himself the vengeance that belongs to God, but he magnified it enormously. He boasted, 'If Cain be avenged sevenfold, then Lamech seventy-sevenfold.'

There is another genealogy in chapter 5, with a very different style, from the hand of P. We will omit it at this point and return to it later when we consider P's understanding of history. From J comes another ancient story at the beginning of chapter 6. The wickedness of the world is now so great that it has corrupted even the 'sons of God'. The story is not easy, especially as it is linked with a tradition about a race of giants. It contains, however, a valuable comment from J, 'The Lord was very sorry that he had made man on the earth, and it grieved him to the heart.' This is J's introduction to the story of the flood.

UNIVERSAL DISASTER AND A NEW BEGINNING

At the end of the last century some clay tablets were discovered at Nineveh dating some two thousand years before Christ. One of these tablets tells the story of a man's search for immortality, and includes a flood which has parallels with the biblical flood of Genesis 9, e.g. the building of an ark, sealing it with bitumen, sending out a raven, and landing on a mountain. Mesopotamia is subject to frequent flooding, and when, earlier this century, evidence was found near Ur of a flood of much greater extent than usual, some people concluded that the biblical flood was a historical occurence. There are, however, stories of floods in the mythologies of Eskimos as well as of Melanesians and the Aborigines of Australia, to name but a few. If these are all based on an historical event the flood must have been of cosmic proportions! Whatever the origin of the story may have been, the accompanying chart shows that the biblical writers have used part of the Babylonian epic for the purpose of showing God's plan for the continuance of the human race through the obedience of individuals.

The J and P passages in the biblical flood account are very cleverly dove-tailed together. It is however, possible to identify them and to find two separate stories each complete in itself, and each agreeing on the

SUMERIAN	BABYLONIAN	J ACCOUNT	P ACCOUNT
The gods decreed destruction of man	Decreed by gods	Yahweh decreed destruction of man for their wickedness	God decreed destruction of all flesh for its corruption
Hero: Ziusandra	Utnapishtim	Noah	Noah
Warning: By Enki in a dream	By Ea in a dream		By voice of God
A huge ship	Ship 120x120x120 7 stories		Ark 300x50x50 3 Stories
	All Kinds of Animals	7 pairs clean, 2 of unclean	2 of all
Floods and storms	Heavy rain and storms	Rain	Rain, and fountains of deep broken
Lasted 7 days	6 days	40 days water subsiding over 2 periods of 7 days	150 days subside in 150 days
	Ship grounds on Mt. Nizir		Grounds on Ararat
	Utnapishtim sends out dove, swallow and raven	Noah sends out dove and raven	
Ziusandra sacrifices to sun-god on ship	Utnapishtim sacrifices on Mt Nizir. The gods gather like flies	Noah offers sacrifice on altar. Yahweh smells the sweet savour	
Ziusandra is granted immortality	Utnapishtim is granted immortality, and his wife, with deification. Ishtar's necklace of lapis lazuli as a sign of remembrance.	Yahweh resolves not to curse ground for man's sake	God makes covenant not to destroy earth again, with rainbow as sign of covenant

9. Chart to show variations in flood stories

main points though differing in detail. That J is incomparably the better story-teller may be seen by looking at his version, which can be found in the following verses: Genesis 7:1–5, 7, 16b, 8–10, 12, 17b, 22–23; 8:6a, 2b, 3a, 6b, 8–12, 13b, 20.

In telling of Noah's sacrifice, J again takes us to the heart of God, who promises never again to destroy the earth. Even though man will continue to sin, God's grace will support him. Even more strongly than in the stories of Cain and Abel, and in spite of the terrible devastation of the flood which was fully deserved, the wonderful saving power of God is J's final word.

Two more tales that J has inherited have to be inserted somewhere, and they fit here very loosely. One is the difficult story of Noah's drunkenness. To him was given a new skill, the cultivation of the vine, and he had to learn its potency. It is inexperience, not depravity that causes his drunkenness. The reaction of Ham—thought to be the ancestor of the Canaanites—is different from that of his brothers, so he is cursed. Here seems to be the rationalization for the Israelites' conquest of the Canaanites.

J's second story, of the tower of Babel, is another example of the disharmony caused by man's pride; the barrier in communication extends so that nation cannot speak to nation. Yet still God's purposes cannot fail; he called one man, and of him made a new tribe. Abraham was called to be the father of Israel. Abraham obeyed God's call, and so again there is hope.

SUGGESTIONS FOR STUDY AND DISCUSSION

1. What myths do you know from other faiths and countries which try to account for the origin of evil?
2. 'Good and evil are inextricably intertwined.' Do you agree?

CHAPTER 5

Patriarchs

Passages for study: Genesis 12–end;
Isaiah 51:1–6; Habakkuk 2:1–5

THE FATHER OF THE JEWS

God is often called 'The God of Abraham, Isaac, and Jacob', who are known as the Patriarchs of Israel. Yet even with Abraham we are not in verifiable history. Archaeologists have found evidence of more than one migration from Mesopotamia to Haran during the second millenium BC; it is a matter of speculation which if any of these is that of the tribal ancestor of Genesis 12. Remembered traditions have clustered about Abraham's name to form not a history, but a saga. There is a second saga, with a slightly different style, about Jacob. Stories about Isaac, who remains a rather shadowy figure, form a link between the two. The last chapters of Genesis are taken up with the romantic tale of Joseph, at the end of which the tribes are a stage further on their journey, in Egypt. These sagas and tales have been put together to form the larger story of the working out of God's purpose. Women seem to have had little choice, yet they are none the less important; the purpose could not have been accomplished without them!

According to J, God called one individual to leave his home and to venture into the unknown, with the consolation only of a distant blessing.

> Now the Lord said to Abram, 'Go from your country and your kindred and your father's house to the land which I will show you. And I will make of you a great nation, and I will bless you and make your name great, so that you will be a blessing. I will bless those who bless you, and those who curse you I will curse; and by you all the families of the earth shall be blessed.' So Abraham went.
>
> *Genesis 12:1–4a*

In our age of great mobility leaving home is a common-place; in the time of Abraham ancestral ties were indissoluble, and God's call involved total commitment. Any ancient stories there may have been about the way in which Abraham's call came, and the immediate reasons for his migration have been forgotten. All that mattered was that God called, and Abraham obeyed. In such a way are God's purposes always fulfilled. The P account of the promise is given in chapter 17; in it Abram's name is changed to Abraham. Scholars have found no significance in the change; it seems to be Ps way of marking the new era which began with Abraham.

God's promise is a recurrent theme throughout Genesis; see also 18:18; 22:18; 26:4; 28:14. The gracious purpose of God is indeed the basis of the whole Pentateuch. The promise is threefold—descendants who will become a great nation, a special relationship with God, and the future possession of land. Genesis is concerned only with the first of these; it closes with the death of Joseph in a foreign land, but with the nucleus of a great nation firmly established in the families of all the sons of Jacob, who became Israel.

THE ESTABLISHMENT OF THE RACE

Many of the best-loved stories in Genesis concern the provision of an heir to the promise—a task often accompanied by great difficulty. Sarah had given up all hope of child-bearing, so she gave her slave Hagar to Abraham, and then after Hagar had given birth to Ishmael, the three visitors came to tell Abraham that he would soon have a son by Sarah. Sarah laughed (Genesis 18). When the promised heir, Isaac, was but a lad, Abraham felt impelled to offer him back to God in the only way he knew, by offering him as a sacrifice. Abraham learnt that this was not what God wanted, and he later went to great lengths to provide a suitable bride for Isaac. The servant's long journey, crowned by the apparently chance meeting of the right girl at the well is in the best tradition of storytelling. All was not happy, however, when Rebecca gave birth to twins who 'quarrelled' even as they left her womb. Rebecca aided Jacob in deceiving his old, blind father in order to gain the birth-right. Jacob fled from his brother's wrath, and spent many years in an alien land before he dared to return. On his way back, he sent two convoys of gifts for Esau, and then sent his wives ahead across the river. Alone, he had to wrestle with an unknown assailant, and in the struggle, he was given a new name, Israel, Prince of God. From Jacob, the promise passed to one of his younger sons, Joseph. The 'coat of many colours' is better translated as a 'long robe with sleeves', a garment which signified that he did not have to labour like his brothers, because he was the heir. Through the treachery of his brothers, once again the heir to the promises had to dwell in an alien land. Joseph prospered in Egypt—until he was betrayed by Potiphar's wife and imprisoned and forgotten for many years. The inheritance seemed still in jeopardy. Only some time after Joseph had been able to interpret the dreams of the Pharaoh was he freed; his brothers and their families joined him in Egypt, and it seemed that at long last the promises might be fulfilled.

REASONS FOR SURVIVAL OF SAGA AND CULT-LEGEND

There are several reasons why these stories have survived while others have been forgotten. One is their appeal to ordinary human experience. Entertaining angels unawares as Abraham did, is a common experience. So is that of being tested to the limit of endurance even when obedience seems to involve giving up hope of promise. Such common experiences are the stuff of saga, even though they are told in such ancient tales that many of the details are meaningless for us today. For example, was Abraham's call to offer Isaac as a sacrifice originally something to do with human sacrifice, which was an accepted practice in some circumstances? (See the moving story of Jephthah's daughter in Judges 11.)

What are we to make of the crippling of Jacob when he struggled all night before he earned the right to be called Israel? Or of the need for the attacker to disappear before daybreak (32:22ff)? As the story is retold by J we are clearly meant to understand that the assailant is the Lord, and many today will sympathize with Jacob's struggle to discover God's name, that is, his nature. But why should God have to be gone before dawn? A late Jewish Midrash suggests that he had to return to heaven to lead the dawn choir. More plausible seems the suggestion that this is a trace of an ancient story about a spirit who made the river crossing specially difficult in the dark. Wesley's hymn beginning, 'Come, O Thou Traveller unknown', indicates the deep significance of the tale.

In vain Thou strugglest to get free,
I never will unloose my hold;
Art Thou the Man that died for me?
The secret of Thy love unfold
Wrestling, I will not let Thee go,
Till I Thy Name, Thy Nature know.

Jacob's earlier encounter with God had been at Bethel, where he had seen angels ascending and descending the heavenly ladder and he had heard the voice of God (Genesis 28:10f). El in both names, Beth-el and Penu-el, is the Canaanite name for the Most High God. This association of places with an unexpected and overwhelming awareness of God is common throughout history. Lourdes is one modern example. In South India it has been possible to watch the development of two such holy sites during the early part of this century, unconcerned with official religion. One was the burial-place of a Christian missionary whose saintliness was recognized by Hindu and Christian alike. His grave became a place of pilgrimage, and eventually a Hindu shrine. Another such shrine grew up on the spot where a man was inexplicably killed by a passing train. At first, drivers threw out coins and flowers; then someone erected a pillar, and prayers became public. The prayers included a recital of the original happening. Such recitals in the course of worship are sometimes called 'cult-legends'. The word legend comes from the same root as legible, and means simply 'that which is read'; there is no suggestion that the tale is imaginary, although there may well be embroidery added in the constant re-telling. There are many tales in Genesis which stem from cult-legends. Many of the places where Abraham built an altar had for long been sacred to the dwellers in the land, for example, the oaks of Moreh near Shechem, and the oaks of Mamre near Hebron (Genesis 12:6; 13:18). Isaac had his encounter with God at the spring of Beer-sheba (26:23–25). These cult-legends provide a second reason for the survival of some tales rather than others.

A third reason for their survival is the simple delight in a good tale. There is much of this in the stories of Jacob's dealings with Laban, and in the story of Joseph, which follows a common folk theme of the heir deprived of his inheritance by jealous brothers and eventually, after many vicissitudes, becoming the means of their salvation. An indication of the popularity of the tale comes from the slight discrepancies within it. For example, was Joseph sold to Midianites or to Ishmaelites? When he finally made himself known to his brothers, did he immediately send for his father, as in 45:9, or did Pharaoh himself make a gracious invitation, as in 45:17? If the latter, then why did Joseph have to introduce his brothers to Pharaoh in the chapter following (46:28–47:4)? The simplest explanation is that the story had been circulating over a wide area for a long time, so that variations have crept in. These details make no difference to the gist of the story, nor to its value. Besides the two sources already mentioned, scholars have suggested another, known as E because it uses the word Elohim for God. It may have been the version circulating in the northern kingdom, possibly written down in the time of Elijah and Elisha. Later on the two sources were combined—in the Joseph story in such a way that it is impossible to see the joins.

There is a folk-tale quality too, about the man who, going to a foreign country is so afraid that others may kill him for the sake of his beautiful wife that he gives her to them readily, pretending she is his sister—in order to save his own skin. Surprisingly it is the very first story we are told about Abraham. Its position just after the account of his call is in stark contrast to his obedience to that call, and brings in the compilers' subsidiary theme of the difficulty in fulfilling the promise. Both famine and lack of faith contributed to the deferment of an heir; yet God does not fail. Pharaoh is punished for his unwitting sin, and Abraham sent on his way with greatly increased wealth. Sarah's part is not commented on!

We are faintly surprised when we meet the same story in chapter 20, with slight variations. This time Abraham was in Gerar, a city near Gaza, and he gave his wife to Abimelech, its king. He behaved exactly as he had done in Egypt, apparently having learned nothing from his earlier experience! Apart from the identity of place and person, and a certain reflective interest, the second story is like the first. The similarity not only of content but of language and style too, suggests to scholars that this is the E version of the same tale. Here it is placed just after the annunciation to Abraham of the birth of Isaac. It must have been an immensely popular tale, for there is yet another version of it in chapter 26. The king is Abimelech as in the second story, but it is Isaac who visits him. It is not easy for modern readers to gain much from the tales themselves, but as the third account follows the birth of the quarrelling twins, the contrast between the promise and its delayed fulfilment is again emphasized.

THE PURPOSE OF GOD

Yet the total impression is of a gradual move towards fulfilment. The skill of the compiler is further shown when Joseph finally revealed himself to his brothers and said that he forgave them; he made it clear that God was in charge.

> God did send you before me to preserve life ... so it was not you
> who sent me here, but God.
>
> *Genesis 45:5*

And again, in the final chapter:

> You meant evil against me, but God meant it for good, to bring it
> about that many people should be kept alive.
>
> *Genesis 50:20*

So the first part of the prose has been fulfilled. When Joseph died his body was embalmed to await the time when it could be carried to the Promised Land.

The great antiquity of some of the material and the variety of sources used provide difficulties which are only incidental to those who read the book not as history, but as the faith of the Jews since the exile. Genesis is part of the Torah, the word of God. It declares that God has a purpose which is being fulfilled, however delayed; his saving power cannot fail (Habakkuk 2:1–5).

PASSAGES OF SPECIAL INTEREST TO CHRISTIANS

For those who read Genesis believing also that the Word of God is revealed in Jesus, there are three passages which are worth special notice. First, there is the High Priesthood of Melchizedek in chapter 14. This is applied to the Davidic dynasty in Psalm 110, and specifically to Jesus in the Epistle to the Hebrews (Hebrews 7:1–10). The whole of this chapter of Genesis is the subject of much discussion. It comes from none of the recognized sources, and seems as out of place as a granite boulder on an alluvial plain. Unlike the peaceful nomad of the rest of Genesis, Abraham appears with a private army to rescue Lot from a confederacy of kings. After his victory he was met by Melchizedek, king of Salem, who feasted him with bread and wine, and then gave him a blessing from 'The Most High God'. Abraham responded by giving to Melchizedek a tithe of what he had gained through his conquest, thus showing his allegiance. While the symbolism is recognizable, the original meaning remains a mystery.

The following chapter, 15, gives what is possibly the E version of Abraham's call, followed by an awe-inspiring ceremony from J during which Abraham waited long beside the carcases of birds and beasts. When the sun had gone down and all was dark, 'a smoking fire and a flaming torch passed between them', and the promise of land was made explicit. (It is worth noting in passing that the extent of the Promised Land is exactly that of Solomon's kingdom as given in 1 Kings 4:21; this supports the theory that J was written then.) The compilers of Genesis have clearly placed this incident, which leads Abraham into a closer relationship with God, immediately after Abraham has renounced a tithe of his gains to the priest of the Most High God. Little is known of this ancient covenant ceremony, although Jeremiah was aware of it (Jeremiah 34:17f). The death of the animals set free the life within them, presumably uniting the parties who are making the covenant, yet bringing a curse on any breach of it. Before the ceremony Abraham had questioned God about his childlessness, and we are told, 'Abraham believed God, and it was reckoned to him for righteousness'. This was a key sentence for Paul, (Romans 4:3) and its key words need explaining. 'Reckoning' or, more precisely, 'imputing', was the word used for the action of the priest when he approved a sacrifice as acceptable to God (Leviticus 7:18). Belief did not mean giving intellectual assent to a statement of doctrine but was an act of trust—a venturing into the unknown in obedience to God's call. Righteousness did not mean attaining perfection in some moral sphere, but was concerned with a right relationship with God. It was no priest who imputed right-eousness to Abraham, but God himself, and it was Abraham's faith that had put him into such a relationship, not any sacrifice he had offered, nor good deed he had done. This is the truth that Paul takes up, that it is a person's right relationship with God built on trust in him which enables God's gracious purposes to be fulfilled.

A third passage which is of special interest because of the way it had been used by Christians is Abraham's entertaining the three strangers who visited him to announce the birth of an heir (Genesis 18). Who were the three? Were they angels or men? Or were they God himself? If God, then why three? The text is far from clear, but there are certain passages in which it is said that the Lord spoke. The Lord told Abraham he would have a son; he rebuked Sarah for her laughter; he warned Abraham of the destruction of Sodom and Gomorrah. And it was the Lord with whom Abraham in his anguish dared to raise questions about the individuals who would suffer with the guilty community, and of whom he said, 'Shall not the Judge of all the earth do right?' The insoluble mystery of the three has been used as an icon of God by the Eastern Church. In the church of San Vitale in Ravenna there is a mosaic of the three figures seated at a table. Their eyes are fixed on

Abraham, and their hands point to his offering. In the later fifteenth century icon of Rublev the figures are still seated, but they are not *behind* the table, but around it; the lines of their robes suggest movement, and the loving glances that pass between them draw in also the spectator. Here is a glimpse of the dance of love, the giving and receiving of love. Stephen Verney writes, 'Through that dance of love there is revealed to us the glory of God. Through that unity which is diversity, and that diversity which is unity, there dawns upon us the mystery of God's name, which is I AM' (from *Christian*, volume 1, number 1).

This is to anticipate 'the reverberations through the ages' which give fuller meaning to the word spoken to Abraham. The next great advance in understanding came through Moses.

SUGGESTIONS FOR STUDY AND DISCUSSION

1. In the light of the Abraham saga what do you understand of the doctrine of 'justification by faith'?
2. Which of the Patriarchal stories would you tell to children? Give reasons.

CHAPTER 6

Moses and the People of God:

I The worshipping community

Passages for study: Exodus 1–15; 22; Hosea 11; Isaiah 43; 44:1–8

Moses is a key figure in the Torah. His importance lies not only in leading the people out of Egypt, but also in the whole idea of Israel as a religious community. When some two thousand years after the Exodus, Sirach wrote his eulogy of 'famous men and women and our fathers in their generations', he said of Moses, 'The Lord brought forth a man of mercy, who found favour in the sight of all flesh . . . beloved of God and man' (Ecclesiasticus 45:1). The first fifteen chapters of Exodus give substance to this summary.

MOSES' FIRST TASK

The first chapter begins where Genesis ended, with the descendants of Jacob in Egypt. It is clear from the first seven verses that far from being a close-knit family of brothers, by the time of Moses they have grown into a collection of loosely connected clans, meeting perhaps at festivals, or in time of need. Hopes of a return to Canaan were fading. It is impossible to identify 'the Pharaoh who knew not Joseph'. The names of the store-cities, Pithom and Raamses, have led many to think that the Pharaoh of the oppression may have been Rameses II, (1389–1226BC). Certainly Rameses' huge building programme would have needed many labourers, but there are other possibilities. Whoever the ruling Pharaoh may have been Moses would have had the difficult task of persuading a powerful and ambitious ruler to part with much of his labour-force. He would also have had to inspire a down-trodden people to leave their familiar homes for the frightening and unknown desert. Only a man of genius could accomplish such a two-fold task.

How does one account for a man of genius? The ancients had no difficulty—he was a man 'brought forth by the Lord'. Folklore is full of tales of miraculous births, as well as of divine preservation of outstanding men. The delightful tale of the threatened infant Moses hidden in the bulrushes by his mother and rescued by a princess of the ruling power enshrines the common folk-lore theme of the future deliverer of his people saved by divine intervention from the tyranny of a cruel oppressor.. Whatever the facts of the case may be, the story holds the important truth that Moses grew up aware of his heritage, yet well versed in the ways of Pharaoh's court, and safe from the persecution his people were enduring. As a young man he showed himself to be a 'man of mercy' when he intervened on seeing some of his brethren beaten up by their Egyptian taskmasters. When he fled to the desert in fear, he rescued some damsels in distress. Their father, a Midianite priest, befriended him, and under Jethro's protection and tutelage, he grew to maturity and in the knowledge of the desert.

MOSES' CALL

In due time Moses had an overwhelming experience of the presence of God, discovering him to be the same God who had appeared to Abraham, to Isaac and to Jacob, who was now calling him to return to Egypt to rescue their descendants. Moses' understandable reluctance to accept God's call is described in chapters 3 and 4. It is written in terms that are reminiscent of the struggles of both Gideon and Jeremiah, and shows the difficulty of accepting a prophetic vocation (Judges 6; Jeremiah 1). Moses produced one reason after another why he should not obey God's call. 'Why me?' 'What shall I say to the people when they question my authority?' Moses' final argument that he was not eloquent was shown to be no reason, merely an excuse. In desperation Moses begged God to send someone else. So God gave him Aaron to be his prophet. Here is the true definition of a prophet, one who speaks for another; Aaron was Moses' prophet, as Moses was God's (Exodus 4:15–16; 3:14–15).

When Moses asked how he should answer those who questioned his authority he was given a new name for God, that is, a new understanding of his nature. Moses was told to say to the children of Israel, 'I AM has sent me.' At the end of this chapter is an extended note about the meaning of this word for God, usually written in the RSV as the LORD, and also about the reasons for its transcription in some places in the King James' version as Jehovah.

The location of the holy mountain where Moses had his revelation of God, and to which he was commissioned to bring the children of Israel is a matter of lively discussion. In the third chapter of Exodus it is called Horeb, as it is in Deuteronomy; elsewhere it is known as Sinai. It was not until the time of the Emperor Justinian (AD527–565) that it became identified with Jebel Musa in the Sinai Peninsula, where Justinian built a monastery. This site is now traditional among Christians, but it is unknown to Jews! A recently published book argues for a location near Kadesh-Barnea, in northern Arabia. We are told that the Israelites spent many years here, and it seems a little odd that having struggled to lead the people so near to the Promised Land, Moses should make them trek all the way back towards Egypt (Numbers 13:26). It was to Arabia that Paul went after his conversion (Galatians 1:17); what more likely place than Moses' holy mountain? Exodus, chapter 19 only makes the problem more difficult. Did the Lord appear in volcanic fire and earthquake, or merely in a violent storm? Compare verses 16 and 18. There are no signs of volcanic activity near Jebel Musa, but there are near Kadesh. Probably we shall never know the answer. One suggestion is that by this time the tribes had separated, no longer travelling together, and that the Sinai tradition belongs to only one of them. The important point is that it was on the holy mountain that Moses received his call, and that it was here that the Israelites were to know themselves as God's people. The Priestly account of Moses' call makes this clear (Exodus 6:6–7):

I am the Lord . . . I will deliver you from bondage, and I will redeem
you with an outstretched arm and with great acts of judgment,
and I will take you for my people, and I will be your God.

THE CROSSING OF THE SEA

Moses' encounter with Pharaoh, and the plagues which led to the Israelites' eventual departure from Egypt, are described in chapters 7–11 and 12:29–39. We will leave their consideration until later, passing to the crucial part of the escape, the crossing of the sea. The actual story of the escape is very confused, and details of the passing through the sea are hard to establish. There is no doubt however, about the fact of the crossing. Psalms 78, 105 and 106 give no details, only the incredible fact.

He rebuked the Red Sea and it became dry; and he led them
through the deep as through a desert.
Psalm 106:9

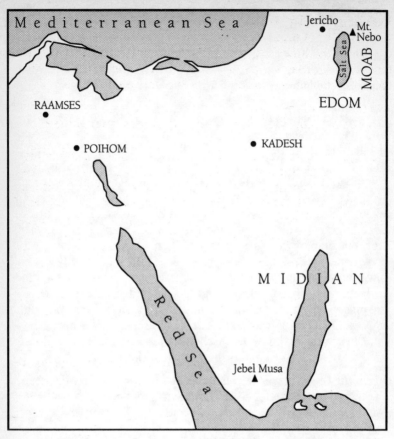

10. Sketch map of area covered by 'wilderness wanderings'

The prophet of the exile, praying for a new exodus, addressed God in faith:

> Was it not thou that didst dry up the sea,
> the waters of the great deep;
> That didst ask of the depths of the sea a way
> for the redeemed to pass over?
>
> *Isaiah 51:10*

The description of the event in Exodus, chapter 14 has three versions of the immediate causes of the waters' receding; Moses was told to stretch forth his rod (v. 16), he stretched out his hand, and, the Lord drove the waters back by a strong east wind all night (v. 21). This idea of wind is confirmed by Miriam's song in 15:21, which was later enlarged in the time of the monarchy into a glorious psalm, (notice v. 14, which mentions Philistines who had not yet appeared on the scene):

> *At the blast of thy nostrils the waters dried up,*
> *Thou didst blow with thy wind and the waters covered them.*

The wind seems to belong to the earliest tradition, as well as being the most likely cause, provided that one remembers that the sea was not the Red Sea as we know it today. The Red Sea is a misnomer, due to a wrong translation; it should be 'the Sea of Reeds'. This may have been in the central area of what is now the Suez Canal, or it may have been nearer the coast of the Mediterranean Sea. Here is another subject for scholarly discussion!

RITES AND CEREMONIES CONNECTED WITH THE EXODUS

The deliverance from Egypt was so fundamental to the Israelites' awareness of themselves as God's chosen people that three of the rites and ceremonies which bind the Jews together to this day are directly connected with it. Instructions for their observance are even written into the Exodus accounts of the events in chapters 12 and 13. These ceremonies are the Redemption of the Firstborn, the Feast of Unleavened Bread, and the Passover.

The Redemption of the Firstborn stems from ancient and almost universal custom, part of the thanksgiving to the gods for first-fruits and for the fertility of the flocks (Exodus 22:29). After the exodus, the first-born were to be offered only to the Lord, and at some time the rite was linked with the death of Pharaoh's eldest son, the event which finally led to the hasty departure from Egypt. When a young mother offered her firstborn son to the Lord, redeeming him with an offering of 'a pair of turtle-doves or two small pigeons' (Luke 2:23f), it was an occasion of great personal thanksgiving, but it was more. It was a reminder of salvation—hope for the future based on the experience of past history.

The Feast of Unleavened Bread occurs at the beginning of barley harvest (Deuteronomy 16:9). It probably originated in an old Canaanite celebration of the baking of the first loaf from the new crop, like the old English Lammas. Today every Jewish housewife ceremonially searches the house lest there be any hidden leaven, for the festival is now linked to the hasty departure from Egypt, and the time when, living as semi-nomads in the wilderness, they ate the 'bread of affliction'. So the celebration has become associated with Passover, which occurs at the same time of the year, and which also celebrates the Exodus.

The Feast of Passover had a separate origin, probably celebrating the birth of the first lambs in a pastoral community. It was and remains, a family festival, requiring neither priest nor altar—with the possible exception of some 150 years between Josiah's reformation and the exile. The idea of keeping it as a memorial, described in the twelfth chapter of Exodus, could have arisen only after the event, and it is unlikely that such detailed instructions could have been given in the haste of departure. It is suggested that the first part of chapter 12 consists of Priestly instructions written down during the exile. Verses 21–24 are obviously earlier. It seems odd that the Lord should need blood on the door-posts to show where his own people lived! Some form of sprinkling on door-post or threshold is common practice among Eastern peoples, originally to keep away evil spirits; there seems to be a relic of this practice in verse 24 with its mention of the 'destroyer'. Still today the Passover is celebrated with a lamb without blemish, with bitter herbs and unleavened bread. Still the youngest person present asks, 'What mean ye by this service?' and the events of the night of deliverance are recited.

Passover is a time of great rejoicing and many psalms and songs have been written for it, including perhaps Miriam's song and Psalms 78 and 105. There is too a delightful parable in which the children learn the subsequent history of their people. It begins:

A kid, a kid, my father bought
for two pieces of money,
A kid, a kid.

Then came the cat, and ate the kid
That my father bought
for two pieces of money.

Then came the dog, and bit the cat,
That ate the kid
That my father bought
For two pieces of money;
A kid, a kid.

The interpretation reads, 'The kid, a clean animal, refers to Israel, the one peculiar people upon earth, which God purchased for himself by means of the two precious tables of the Law (Exodus 15:16). The cat refers to Babylon which swallowed up Jewish nationality, and the dog means Persia, by whose power Babylon was overthrown.' Next comes the staff, for Greece, the fire for Rome, and water representing the Turks; the ox stands for the western nations which in the latter days rescued the Holy Land from the Turks. The whole, long recital is built up step by step, until a stanza beginning with the slaying of the ox:

Then came the butcher, and slew the ox
That drank the water,
That quenched the fire,
That burnt the staff,
That beat the dog
That bit the cat
That ate the kid
That my father bought
For two pieces of money,
A kid, a kid.

The butcher refers to a fearful war in which the western nations will be driven out; he is followed by the Angel of Death, a pestilence destroying all Israel's enemies, and finally God's kingdom is established on earth under one Messiah, he Son of David.

Then came the Holy One, blessed be He!
And killed the Angel of Death,
That killed the butcher
That slew the ox ... and so on.

These verses are found in the *Seder Hagadah*, (Passover Service book) and are translated from the Aramaic. They are included here to illustrate both the Jewish love of story and parable, and also the joy of recital.

THE PLAGUES

Recital has coloured the way in which the story of the plagues has been preserved. They make dramatic reading aloud, with their repetition of certain phrases, and their constant pattern. 'The Lord said to Moses, "Go to Pharaoh and say to him, Thus says the Lord, the God of the Hebrews, Let my people go that they may serve me."' Pharaoh refuses, the plague falls. Then Pharaoh, humbled, asks Moses to beg God to remove the plage; Moses concedes, the plague is stayed, but Pharaoh's heart is hardened. There are interesting variations from this basic pattern. Furthermore, while Exodus describes ten plagues, there are only seven in the Psalms. Apart from differences in language which are not always obvious in translation, there are also differences in the ways in which the plagues are brought about. In some we are told simply that the Lord acted (8:24) whereas in others Moses is the intermediary, stretching out his hand, or his rod, or throwing dust into the air; sometimes it is Aaron who is the intermediary. Some of the plagues come through one method only, some through two, and in some there are references to all three. Here again is a mixture of different traditions. Those mentioning Aaron are probably from the Priestly tradition, the simplest are probably the earliest, J. In E the magical element of the rod is beginning to appear. There may well have been confusion between lice and flies as well as between diseases of men and cattle as the tales were repeated in various localities and in successive ages. The editors have made a patchwork of all the traditions, which are very difficult to disentangle. One attempt to do so is given below.

	J	E	P
1	Nile smitten	Nile turned to blood	Nile turned to blood
2	Frogs	——	Frogs
3	——	——	Lice (Mosquitoes)
4	Flies	——	——
5	Murrain on cattle	——	——
6	——	——	Boils on man and beast
7	Hail	Hail	——
8	Locusts	Locusts	——
9	Darkness	Darkness	——
10	Firstborn	Firstborn	Firstborn

11. Sources of the plague stories

Each plague is of course, a natural disaster, and some follow naturally upon others. For example, a plague of flies comes as no surprise after piles of frogs had been left lying around! The miracle occurs partly in their cumulative coincidence, but even more in the presence and persistence of Moses. Yet although the plagues were brought about directly by Moses, the editors leave us in no doubt that the Lord is in charge—even to the hardening of Pharaoh's heart. Gradually Pharaoh seemed to make concessions, and at last he agreed that the men should be allowed to leave. When Moses insisted that women and flocks should go as well it was clear that a total withdrawal was intended, and again Pharaoh hardened his heart. The recital now becomes a confrontation between Pharaoh and Moses, between king and pro-phet. Such confrontation arose often during the course of Israel's history, for example, between David and Nathan, Ahab and Elijah, Jeroboam II and Jeremiah, and, too, between Pilate and Jesus. The incredible stories of the 'wonders' which Moses and Aaron performed before Pharaoh described in chapter 4, verses 1–8, epitomize their struggle. Behind the first magic event lies the idea that the serpent which formed part of Pharaoh's sceptre was a symbol of his power. Moses' power was simply in his shepherd's crook, his rod, yet this was more powerful than all the might of Pharaoh because it was God-given. It is the priestly account which places the rod in the hands of Aaron rather than of Moses. The second sign of the leprous hand is explained in the text itself; the first showing of power is not enough to convince.

In the first chapter of Exodus it is written twice that the children of Israel 'served Pharaoh with rigour'. Moses was told to bring them to serve *God* upon the holy mountain, and the request for service is many times repeated in the following chapters. The supremacy of the Lord is paramount; everything in the recital ministers to this, and to the belief that Israel had been specially called to God's service.

Before the wonder of their deliverance, and the glory of their redeemer, the details of isolated events fade into insignificance. In the words of the Psalmist,

> The Lord brought his people out with joy, and his chosen with thanksgiving.
>
> Psalm 105:43

So Passover is always a feast of great thanksgiving. Yet it is more than a pious remembrance.

It is a celebration of the 'ever-recurrent realization of being the people of God. Every celebrating generation becomes united with the first generation and with all those who have followed. As in that night all families united into the living people, so in the Passover night the generations of the people united together, year after year' (Martin Buber, *Moses*).

NOTES ON THE NAME OF GOD

1. I AM (Exodus 3:14)

A comparison of various English translations shows there are problems.

The King James' version reads I AM THAT I AM

The Revised Version (1884) has I AM THAT I AM, but adds variant readings in the margin, viz:

I AM BECAUSE I AM or

I AM WHO I AM or

I WILL BE WHAT I WILL BE.

RSV and Common Bible read I AM WHO I AM, and give alternative readings as a footnote, viz:

I AM WHAT I AM or

I WILL BE WHAT I WILL BE.

The Hebrew letters translated I AM, and the closely related consonants YHWH are both connected with the verb HAYAH, to be. Their exact meaning remains a subject of discussion. Some have argued that the best translation is 'I am he who is'; others say, 'I am who I am'; still another possibility is that the verb may be causative, i.e., to cause to be. Hence the Hebrew words could mean that God is the creator, the source of all being, that he himself is All-Being; that he is the cause of all that occurs and that therefore his purposes cannot fail; or they may mean simply that he will allow no further knowledge of himself—he is beyond the understanding of man. Every parent and teacher knows that to call a child's name is to demand his immediate attention; to know the name gives power. Which particular interpretation is important for any generation depends on the philosophy by which it lives. For the Hebrews the vital element was the continuing presence of the God who had promised Abraham both a special relationship with himself and the possession of land. This has been made clear in the preceding verse, 12. 'The Lord, the God of your fathers, the God of Jacob, has sent me unto you.' Whatever else YHWH means it indicates the continuous presence of God, who remembers his promise to Abraham, and so it includes the ideas of redemption and adoption. The book of Exodus is concerned with both of these ideas, which are inherent in the promise of a special relationship between God and his people. In the words of Bishop David Jenkins, God is Presence, Purpose, Promise and Power.

2. Jehovah

To understand how YHWH came to be read as Jehovah, (and, surprisingly, still is, in the NEB) it is necessary to understand both the Hebrew reverence for the divine name, and also something of the way Hebrew was written. To speak about God as we have so often been doing in these chapters is automatically to make him an object outside ourselves, as when two people speak together about a third who is not present. If God is indeed the great I AM, then in him we live and move and have our being; to speak about him is to ignore this truth. The Jews know this; they will not speak his name. Whenever the divine name YHWH occurs in reading, Jews will substitute for it, ADONAI, the Lord, acknowledging his Lordship with bowed heads. Since after the scattering of the people at the time of the Babylonian conquest Hebrew ceased to be a spoken language, people forgot how to pronounce YHWH; Yahweh is the usual guess. Ancient Hebrew was written with consonants only. For single words there might seem confusion, but usually the context makes the meaning clear, especially when the passage is familiar through frequent reading. Take as an example the letters LRD. They may be read as Lord, lard, lurid or loured, but there can be no doubt of their meaning in the following sentence:

TH LRD S M SHPHRD

When the Torah was translated curious mistakes were sometimes made by using the wrong vowels. Saint Jerome (c. AD400) commenting on Genesis 15:11, wrote that his copy of the Septuagint told that Abraham, instead of 'driving the fowls away' actually sat down with them; the consonants are the same. Where there are unresolved discrepancies the translators have to make a choice; this is why variant readings sometimes are given in footnotes. In Genesis 46:28, for example, the RSV tells us that Jacob sent Judah before him to Joseph 'to appear before him in Goshen'. A note tells us that this is the reading of the Samaritan text, whereas the Hebrew and the Vulgate read, 'to show him the way to Goshen.' To obviate the difficulties caused by substituting the wrong vowels, a group of Jewish scholars produced an authoritative copy of the Scriptures in which symbols rather like an English apostrophe were placed between the consonants; this is known as the Massoretic Text. Like all good Jews, the Massoretes said Adonai instead of the name given to Moses, and they wrote the vowels they actually spoke over the consonants they dared not utter. So, using English symbols, instead of Hebrew, the name of God is written YaHoWaiH; this Christian translators wrote as Jehovah, a word unknown to Jews. It is now usually transcribed as the LORD, as always in the RSV.

3. The name of God in the priestly tradition (Exodus 6:2–8)

Observant readers will have noticed that whereas in some chapters of Genesis the word used for the creator is the Lord, in others it may be God, the Lord God or God Almighty. These represent names which were common among all Canaanite peoples. The P source is punctilious about not using YHWH until it is given to Moses. We can therefore assume that any passage before Exodus 6 which contains 'the Lord' is not from the Priestly source. In P's account of the call of Moses, there is no indication of his prophetic role, since P is more interested in Aaron than in Moses. Surprisingly, for P, the call is in Egypt, not on the holy mountain.

4. Speaking about God

Although in God 'we are all in him enclosed', there are occasions when we need to speak of him as distinct from his creation. There is difficulty here in the use of a pronoun, as English has no personal pronoun which does not also connote gender. God's relationship with his people is such that an impersonal pronoun would be as wrong as one which indicates either a male or female. The way out of the difficulty chosen here is to continue to use the traditional 'he', but to note at this point that to do so is not to indicate the gender of God.

SUGGESTIONS FOR STUDY AND DISCUSSION

1. Find out all you can about the Jewish Passover celebrations.
2. Why do Easter hymns refer so often to the Passover and exodus?
3. Moses was instrumental in interpreting the exodus. In view of Joel 2:28 and Acts 2:1, 28 do you think the Church should inherit the role of Moses? In this connection what do you understand by the Church?

CHAPTER 7

Moses and the People of God:

II The covenant in Exodus

Passages for study: Exodus 16–24; 32–34; Amos 5;
Jeremiah 31:29–34

JOURNEY THROUGH THE WILDERNESS

The compilers of the Book of Exodus show us that after Moses had led his rabble across the Sea of Reeds, God was completely in charge. Three days travelling through the wilderness brought the Israelites to water, but, alas, it was too brackish to drink. Not surprisingly, they grumbled at Moses, who, again not surprisingly, cried to the Lord. The Lord showed Moses a tree whose branches would heal the waters. Some time afterwards, the whole expedition came to a larger oasis where they settled for a time.

Soon they were murmuring again, this time about the dullness of the food after the flesh-pots of Egypt—and the Lord sent manna. Later came fresh murmuring about the shortage of water, recorded in chapter 17. Here there is evidence of the artistry of the compilers, whether conscious or not. In verse 2 the complaint is stated, and in the following verse reiterated from another source. The repetition has the effect of making the grumbling into a real dispute between Moses and the people as well as showing a lack of faith in God. Moses called the place Meribah, which means striving. The people had said to Moses, 'Why have you brought us out of the land of Egypt to kill us with thirst?' Behind this is a deeper question, 'Is the Lord with us or not?' So Meribah and Massah (the name given to it in the Book of Numbers) are remembered as a place of faithlessness:

> O that today you would hearken to his voice!
> Harden not your hearts, as at Meribah,
> as on that day at Massah in the wilderness,

When your fathers tested me,
and put me to the proof, though they had seen my work.

Psalm 95:7–9

Two other incidents of the desert journey are recorded in Exodus, the battle of the Amalekites, in which Moses is recognized as leader, and the family interlude of Jethro's visit. He came to meet Moses, bringing with him Moses' two sons Gershom and Eliezer, as well as Zipporah, Moses' wife. The sons take no further part in the story, but their names mentioned here serve to remind us of Moses' flight from Egypt and his preparation in the wilderness for his great task. Moses and Jethro rejoiced together over God's goodness. After Jethro had given Moses advice about his problems, he returned to Midian, and Moses continued to lead the people to the holy mountain.

MAKING THE COVENANT

Chapter 19 gives an account of the climax of all their wanderings through the desert. Here, on the holy mountain where Moses had received his call, the Lord appeared again in earthquake, storm, wind and fire, and all the people trembled in awe. Here, we are told, they accepted his covenant, saying, 'All that the Lord has spoken we will do.' The glorious words introducing the covenant are not a verbatim report of actual words heard by Moses. How could they be? They do, however, describe the inner meaning of the covenant as understood by later generations of holy men.

You have seen what I did to the Egyptians, and how I bore you on eagles' wings and brought you to myself. Now therefore if you will obey my voice and keep my covenant, you shall be my own possession among all peoples; for all the earth is mine, and you shall be to me a kingdom of priests and a holy nation.

Exodus 19:4–6

These words are a trumpet call to later generations, a reminder to those for whom the compilers were writing, and for all later readers, of their great heritage, their high calling to be the people of God. Here is the vision the compilers would have us share with them.

A covenant in its simplest form is a solemn agreement between two parties. When David had to leave the court because of Saul's jealousy, he made a covenant with Jonathan before the Lord; to break the covenant meant death, so binding was it (1 Samuel 20:16). To illustrate the binding nature of a covenant, in one of his sermons to undergraduates Austin Farrer described two Arab sheiks making an agreement about the boundaries of their grazing lands. He said that having made their decisions, they would 'solemnly eat from one dish, the flesh of the same goat or ram would become in part the flesh of them both, this would make them brothers; but if they were to eat the ram they must kill it first, and here is another opportunity for finalizing the covenant. For killing is a finality. As they cut the ram's throat each of them says, "The Lord do so to me and worse, if I abide not by this covenant." Then they dip their fingers into the blood and touch their bodies with it to apply the force and finality of death to themselves.' Today we no longer sign in blood, but the seals we put on our solemn documents are always red! Covenants are also made between nations and between one nation and a vassal state. The discovery of ancient tablets containing the terms of such covenants have led many to believe that they may have influenced the form of the Ten Commandments. Be that as it may, there is no doubt that the compilers of Exodus wanted their readers to understand that being the people of God involves not only a recognition of all that God has done for them in the past, but also an obedience to his will for them in the present, so that as a kingdom of priests they might serve his eternal glory.

A careful reading of chapters 19 and 20, which describe the covenant-making, shows that the narrative is not continuous, but is composed of strands of different traditions. The feeling of awe is thereby intensified. Still further strands are found in chapter 24, all describing events on the holy mountain. Did Moses go alone up the mountain, or did he take with him seventy elders? A comparison of verses 2, 9, 14 and 16 in chapter 24 shows different recollections; we cannot know precisely what occurred. Yet from the differing traditions some important ideas emerge. Moses may have been the spokesman and mediator of the covenant, but it was made, not with Moses alone, but with all the people, represented by the seventy elders. These men had a vision of the glory of God, and contrary to popular expectation, did not die as a result. They also shared a meal in the presence of God. Another aspect of covenant-making appears in verse 3, where the blood which seals the covenant was sprinkled on the altar, and on the people. Thus the finality of the covenant is underlined.

WHAT HAPPENS IF MEN BREAK THE COVENANT

Looking quickly through the rest of Exodus, we see that chapters 20–23 contain laws and ordinances which we will consider later, and chapters 25–31 and 34, contain instructions for worship. These include recipes for holy oil as well as for building the ark, instructions for making all the fitments of the tabernacle where God may dwell with his people— curtains, high-priestly garments—together with rules for consecrating priests. Much of this is not contemporary, but is the vision of the priests of the exile who were longing for a restoration of and perfection in worship. There is a startling break in the instructions in chapters 32– 34, a break so dramatic that it is certain that these chapters are of vital importance and another facet of the compilers' total vision. According to these chapters Moses remained on the mountain so long that the people grew impatient, and persuaded Aaron to make a golden calf which they immediately worshipped. Aaron's compliance is another surprise; surely the spokesman and leader of their religion should have known better! Once more, the details of what actually happened are not clear. Some of the material is early, but it contains contradictions. For example, did the Lord *tell* Moses what had happened, as in verse 7, or did Moses discover it for himself, as verse 17 implies? These differences are, of course, insignificant in view of the total picture the compilers have produced.

The terrifying God of chapters 19 and 20 shows here another aspect of his nature; in response to Moses' pleading he revealed himself as a God of forgiveness and renewal. The children of Israel had broken the covenant completely and utterly; forgetting the God who brought them out of the land of Egypt, they had worshipped a graven image. According to the terms of the covenant they should have died.

Whatever actually happened in the wilderness, the story is a parable of the later history of the nation. The early traditions had been studied and combined during the exile, the time of great heart-searching by those who struggled to understand the disaster which had befallen them. The worship of the golden calves put up by Jeroboam was seen as the cause of their downfall.

Amos saw that worship itself could be a cause of sin if it did not include obedience to God's law. Justice also was necessary. Amos said, in the reign of Jeroboam II,

> I hate, I despise your feasts,
> and I take no delight in your solemn assemblies;
> Even though you offer me your burnt-offerings and your
> cereal-offerings
> I will not accept them ...
> But let justice roll down like waters,
> and righteousness like an ever-flowing stream.

Amos 5:21–24

Even Amos, for all his insight into the disasters that were about to befall Israel, could plead with the Lord,

> O Lord God, forgive, I beseech thee,
> how can Jacob stand,
> he is so small!

Amos 7:2

And he called on Israel to repent

> Seek the Lord and live ...
> Seek good and not evil, that you may live,
> and so the Lord, the God of hosts will be with you,
> as you have said;
> Hate evil, and love good,
> and establish justice in the gate;
> it may be that the Lord, the God of hosts,
> will be gracious to the remnant of Joseph.

Amos 5:6, 14–15

THE *HESED* OF GOD

Hosea took further the idea of God's care for Israel:

> When Israel was a child I loved him.
> and out of Egypt I called my son ...
> I led them with cords of compassion
> with the bands of love ...
> How can I give you up, O Ephraim!
> How can I hand you over, O Israel?

Hosea 11:1, 4, 8

71

The northern kingdom fell as Amos had foreseen, and the Assyrians came to the very gates of Jerusalem. The reforms of Hezekiah and Isaiah brought no permanent change; the repentance of the people was 'as the morning dew'. So Jerusalem was captured by the Babylonians in 586BC. Yet the prophets' faith in the steadfast love of God was so sure that Jeremiah who lived through the period of siege and conquest was inspired to prophesy a new covenant (Jeremiah 31:31f). Israel had broken the covenant irreparably, but God does not fail.

Yahweh, the great I AM, is unchanging; his covenant-love is constantly redeeming and renewing. The Hebrew word for covenant-love, *hesed*, has no English equivalent, and translators have struggled to find a suitable word for it. The King James' version, mercy, is inadequate; to our Western ears it contains an element of condescension which is lacking in the Hebrew. *Hesed* springs from an inner loyalty to the covenant, which is more than a formal agreement. Faithfulness, loving-kindness, mercy, are all part of it, but none by itself gives the idea of the intense personal relationship of God with his people which the prophets saw as the core of the covenant. The RSV translates *hesed* by 'steadfast love'.

DETAILED REGULATIONS FOR LIVING THE COVENANT

The peoples' part of the covenant was obedience to the will of God, to the Torah. Chapter 20–23 of the Book of Exodus is sometimes known as the book of the covenant as it contains the key obligations. It begins with the Ten Commandments, (in Greek, the Decalogue). These are prefaced with a reminder of what God has done for his people, and consist of a series of commands each beginning with a personal pronoun—'You shall...' In chapter 34 when the broken covenant was renewed, the Lord said to Moses, 'Cut two tablets of stone like the first, and I will write upon the tables the words which were on the first stones which you broke.' But the words which follow are not exactly those of the Ten Commandments as we might expect. Commands there are, but many of these are concerned with worship. The discrepancy is perhaps due to the addition of other laws to the original Mosaic Law to meet changing conditions. This would account for the fact that the laws in chapter 34 seem to belong to the time when the Israelites were settling into Canaan, and were tempted to worship Canaanite gods. For example, 'You shall tear down their pillars, and cut down their Asherim... lest you make a covenant with the inhabitants of the land' (vv. 13–15). The ordinances in chapters 20–23, on the other hand, seem more relevant to a settled agricultural population, belonging more to the conditions under which Amos and Hosea prophesied. Once again we have to admit a problem over which experts continue to puzzle.

Apart from regulations about feasts and rituals, the ordinances in chapters 20–23 concern different aspects of everyday life. They are markedly lacking in any kind of class distinction; each man is of equal value in the sight of God. (Man in this context means not mankind, but the male of the species; in Hebrew society the woman had no legal status.) The law of revenge in chapter 21:23f is sometimes misread as justifying brutality; in fact it limits it. Whereas Lamech wanted to be avenged seventy-times seven, the Law limits retribution to one bruise for one bruise.

Sternness there is in these laws, and some infringements are punishable by death, but the general tone of this code and of that in chapter 34 is much more lenient than English law in the nineteenth century, and our inner cities today still testify to our failure to care for the poor and needy! Restitution rather than retribution is the underlying principle, recognizing all men as the children of God. The picture of God in Exodus 34:6–7 surely owes much to the prophets:

> The Lord, the Lord, a God merciful and gracious, slow to anger, and abounding in steadfast love and faithfulness, keeping steadfast love for thousands, forgiving iniquity and transgression and sin, but who will by no means clear the guilty, visiting the iniquity of the fathers upon the children and the children's children, to the third and fourth generation.

The tension between God's mercy and his justice appears strongly in the accounts of Moses' meetings with God written in chapter 33. The whole chapter is woven from different sources, but the overall pattern is clear. God repeated his promises of land, but told Moses that because of the peoples' sin he himself would not accompany them thither. Hearing this the people 'stripped off their ornaments'. With this sign of their sorrow Moses again went to the Lord who spoke to him as was his custom, 'as a man speaks to a friend'. Moses' intercession allowed the Lord to show his 'goodness'. 'I will be gracious to whom I will be gracious, and will show mercy on whom I will show mercy.' Yet not even Moses was allowed to see further into the mystery of God. God sheltered him in a rock, and God's hand protected him from the full vision of the glory which was more than mortal man could bear.

SUGGESTIONS FOR STUDY AND DISCUSSION

1. Most children recognize justice; can you explain 'mercy' to them?
2. In what ways do the laws of our land today fall short of the covenant standard?
3. Is there anything in the worship of your parish church which may lead to false worship?
4. Use for meditation some of the titles by which the Psalmists address God.

CHAPTER 8

The Priestly Response to Failure

Passages for study: Exodus 25-31; 35-40;
Ezekiel 37; 40

RELIGION DURING THE EXILE

Whether they be Indians or Bengalis in Bradford, or English in Saudi Arabia, all aliens in a foreign country tend to congregate together. Differences between them and their hosts assume disproportionate importance; lines of separation become more clearly defined. In the same way Jews taken to Babylon after 586BC kept together, thereby maintaining their identity. Added to their absence from home was the devastating knowledge of the total defeat of their country. The learned and the devout amongst them were aware of themselves as God's people, and knew that their disaster was due to the failure of their community to live according to his will. Yet they were deprived of the one place where, according to the Law, they might offer their gifts before the Lord as a token of their repentance (Leviticus 1:5, 11). How could they sing the Lord's song in a strange land (Psalm 137)? Before the exile, to seek God was to visit his sanctuary, as is evidenced by the early Psalms.

Sing praise to the Lord who dwells in Zion,
In Salem is his Tabernacle
and his dwelling in Zion.

Psalm 76:2. See also Psalm 9:11; 48:1-2; 46:4

PLANS FOR RESTORATION OF WORSHIP

The thoughts of those exiles who had spent their lives in the service of the sanctuary, naturally turned to making plans for perfecting worship whenever the return promised by Jeremiah and Ezekiel should occur. Ezekiel himself was a priest, and the last part of his book, from chapter 40 onwards, in concerned with plans for rebuilding Jerusalem and restoring right worship. The closing words of his prophecy re-assert the importance of Jerusalem as the city where God dwells; they have inspired hopes of a return for many generations of Jews as well as providing for Christians a vision of the heavenly Jerusalem. Since the temple, rebuilt under Haggai, and again much more grandly under Herod the Great, was finally destroyed by the Romans in AD70, it has ceased to be a place of worship for the Jews. There is therefore no need here for a detailed reading of those chapters of Ezekiel, nor Exodus 25–31 and 35–40 since they refer to obsolete ways of worship. We saw in the previous chapter that the story of the golden calf and the consequent renewal of the covenant was a parable of Israel's history. It need not surprise us therefore to discover that there is a great similarity in the chapters in Exodus which precede it and those that follow. Chapters 25–31 contain detailed instructions for making, furnishing and maintaining the tabernacle; from 35 onwards these instructions are carried out by the inspired skill of Bezalel and his craftsmen—presumably as a result of the new covenant. The two sections are so much alike that we may surely recognize the work of editors. Here, as in other parts of Exodus, we have a closely woven mixture from the P source, of ancient tradition with exilic hopes for the future, and it is not always easy to disentangle the various threads.

THE TENT OF MEETING AND THE TABERNACLE

It is very difficult to believe that Moses wrote down during the time in the desert such detailed instructions for the construction and furnishing of the tabernacle as we find here, or that all the materials listed would have been available. The priests however knew that right worship stemmed from the idea of the Jews as a worshipping community, and this is the reason for setting their instructions in the framework of the covenant. It seems likely that the account as we have it today is coloured by recollections of Solomon's temple. Be that as it may, the basic idea of a tent of meeting is ancient. It is mentioned three times in chapters 25–31, each time in connection with Moses' function as mediator between God and his people—in 25:22, in 29:43, and in 30:6, 36. The tent seems to have been primarily a place where Moses 'met' God, and was a continuation of God's presence on Sinai. This is made explicit in 34:34, after the account of the renewal of the covenant. A recognizably early fragment in chapter 33, verses 7–11, states the function of the tent, and tells us too that the tent was outside the camp. Joshua was left in charge when Moses was absent. In this tradition,

Moses is the mediator between God and his people, fulfilling his function as God's spokesman, his prophet.

Another tradition has become inextricably entwined with this idea of the tent as a place of meeting with God, that of its being his sanctuary, where only priests and Levites may serve. (Joshua, Moses' servant in the earlier tradition, was an Ephraimite.) The Book of Numbers, also from P, has the tabernacle tradition also; it tells us that eight thousand, five hundred and fourscore Levites were involved in the service of the tabernacle, in its worship and its transport from place to place (Numbers 4:48; 3:5–9)! Behind these obvious exaggerations in the numbers of tabernacle ministers as well as in the elaboration of the furnishings, there is probably a sound tradition of a tent which served a a holy place. The tradition demonstrates two important truths which the Priestly writers have emphasized; one is the holiness of God, and the other his dwelling 'in the midst of' his people. Whereas the tent of meeting was outside the camp, the tabernacle is central to it. The supreme Creator of the universe is so awe-ful and glorious that his creatures may approach him only with the utmost reverence. All the elaboration of the tabernacle is directed to this end.

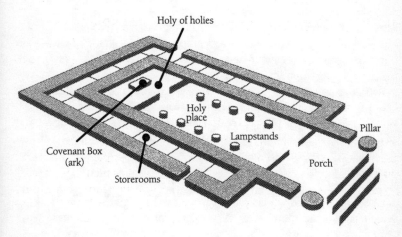

12. Plan of Solomon's temple
(compare the three chambers with the wilderness tabernacle)

As in Solomon's temple, there was a holy place, separated by a veil from an inner, 'most holy', place (Exodus 26:31f). This was the veil which according to Matthew was rent in two at the crucifixion of Jesus (Matthew 27:51). The important figure in this tradition is Aaron the priest rather than Moses. He wore a breastplate bearing twelve jewels, to represent the twelve tribes of Israel when he entered the holy place to offer worship on their behalf. He wore too a gold band on his mitre bearing the words, 'Holy to the Lord' (Exodus 28:15–21, 35–38). The aweful holiness of God was emphasized by the warnings of death to those who approached the sanctuary unworthily; the story of Nadab and Abihu in Leviticus 10 is a solemn cautionary tale.

SYMBOLS OF THE PRESENCE OF GOD

Yet this holy God had promised his presence with his people; to remind them of this was the purpose of the sanctuary (25:8; 29:45). The early traditions told of a pillar of cloud by day, and of fire by night leading the Israelites in their perilous passage to the Sea of Reeds. This may well have been a brazier such as the Bedouin used to carry when on the march. Its purpose was to honour exalted persons, and so from the beginning may have been a reminder that the Lord was with them. By the time the E tradition was written down, the cloud not only 'accompanied them', it 'descended'; in P it has become a fiery cloud, first on Mount Sinai, and then over the tabernacle (Exodus 13:21, 22; 33:9; 40:34–38). Always it is a symbol of the presence of God. God 'dwells' above the heavens he has created; he 'tabernacles' with men. P is careful not to detract from the majesty of God, nor to limit him to any particular place of permanent abode. The symbol of the cloud occurs throughout the Scriptures. It was the cloud of God's presence which filled Solomon's temple, and which, later, Ezekiel saw departing from it (1 Kings 8:10, 11; Ezekiel 10:3, 4). Daniel saw in a vision 'one like a son of man coming on the clouds of heaven' (Daniel 7:13). Here is yet another example of 'the reverberation down the ages' of a word spoken in the past!

Another symbol which comes from the Exodus description of the tabernacle is the 'mercy-seat'. This was a slab of pure gold covering the ark of the covenant, and on it were the cherubim. This was the place where God would commune with his people (Exodus 25:17, 22). Aaron was commanded to make atonement at the mercy-seat after the death of his two sons, and the final part of the ceremony was the sprinkling of blood upon it (Leviticus 16:2, 13–26). So the idea of atonement became associated with the action of the priest, and in the Greek Bible the Hebrew word was translated *hilasterion* which has the connotation of propitiation. The English 'mercy-seat', which was first used by Coverdale following Luther's *gnadenstuhl*, restores the emphasis from the action of a priest to the grace of God. The name fits very well into the interpretation of Christ's death in the Epistle to the Hebrews (9:5). The cherubim, which may have been winged sphinxes, common in Phoenician art, probably provided the throne for the invisible Lord, in much the same way as did Jeroboam's bulls.

One other point about the building of the tabernacle that is worth making, is the involvement of the people in providing the materials. Everyone 'whose heart was willing' was asked to give. 'And they came, everyone whose heart stirred him, and everyone whose spirit moved him', both men and women, bringing brooches and all sorts of gold objects, and silk, linen or fabric of goats' hair, as well as their skills. So much was brought, we are told, that the craftsmen told Moses they had more than enough, and Moses gave orders for the gifts to stop (35:5, 21–29; 36:5–7)!

13. *Sketch of ivory plaque from Ahab's palace in Samaria showing Phoenician style 'cherub'*

P'S USE OF NUMBERS

In the account of the building of the tabernacle, the numbers 3, 4 and 10 frequently occur. This interest in numbers may be the clue to P's peculiar use of numbers elsewhere. The same Hebrew characters are used both for letters and for numbers, and the characters which read 'the children of Israel' add up to 630,000. Is the number of men who crossed the Red Sea an approximation of this (Exodus 12:37)? The number as it stands is clearly impossible. A population of 600,000 men would have also large numbers of women and children, apart from elderly and infirm; a total of two million is the common estimate of the total numbers. This is almost ten times the combined population of Oxford and Reading. The mechanics of taking such a crowd across the sea in a single night would baffle the best authorities on crowd control! Mathematicians might like to work out the size of a regimented column of such magnitude; organizers of festivals might be more interested in human problems, not least in sanitation.

P's peculiar use of numbers also occurs in the genealogies in Genesis. The genealogy in Genesis chapter 5 is P's list of Noah's predecessors. Although Cain is omitted, there is a curious resemblance between this list and J's list of the descendants of Cain which is given in chapter 4, verses 17–23. There is also a resemblance to an ancient list of kings which has been uncovered in Babylonia; there are the same number as in P, and many of the names are the same. In the Babylonian list the seventh king, Enosh, was carried away into the gods and so shared their secrets, like Enoch who 'walked with God'. The tenth in both lists was the hero of the flood. What strikes most people on reading P's genealogy is the great ages of the men, and especially the age at which they begat sons! Methuselah, for example, begat his first son when he was one hundred and eighty-seven years old, and lived for a further seven hundred and eighty-two years. We have no clue to the ancient way of reckoning ages, but we do know that longevity was a sign of God's blessing. P seems to be writing of a golden age. If we take these numbers literally and according to our understanding of years, then, as Martin Luther remarked, nine patriarchs would have been living at the same time. Seth, Adam's son, would have outlived the flood! Ages decrease in later genealogies and in the Samaritan Pentateuch they are more clearly delineated to show a gradual reduction in years. In marked contrast to the first period, the ages from Noah to Abraham are a mere two hundred to six hundred years, from Abraham to Moses one hundred to two hundred, and after Moses until the present day seventy to eighty years. One suggestion is that as P has no account of the origin of evil, the decreasing life-span is a means of showing the gradual fall of mankind. There is a wonderful field for speculation here (Genesis 10; 25:12f; Exodus 6:14f)! There is however, another idea behind these decreasing life-spans; they help to differentiate four periods into which the Priestly writers divided history. These epochs are characterized by other differences, shown as follows:

The priestly view of history

1 From the creation to the flood
The supreme God, known as Elohim, gives man dominion over the earth. Man's life span varies from nine hundred and sixty nine (Methuselah) to a mere three hundred and sixty five (Enoch, who walked with God).

2 From Noah to Abraham
God makes a covenant with all men never again to destroy the earth. God's sign is the rainbow, man's is sacrifice. Ages vary between six hundred and two hundred years.

3 From Abraham to Moses
The names used for God are more personal, e.g. the God of Abraham. That used for the God who makes the covenant with Abraham is El Shaddai, which is the name by which the supreme deity was known in Haran, the part of the Middle East whence Abraham had journeyed. Man's sign is circumcision. The average ages of the patriarchs of this period are one to two hundred years (Genesis 25:12–20; 35:28; Exodus 6:14f.).

4 From Moses to the present day
God reveals his Name, YHWH, to Moses, and renews his covenant with Abraham's descendants, all Israel. Man's sign is the sabbath; God's, his continued presence. This period will end with the coming of the Messiah, and so for Jews lasts until the present day. Man's life-span is seventy to eighty years.

The priestly writers were so certain that the covenant continued to be the basis of Israel's life that every ordinance was ascribed directly to Moses, even those which were promulgated during the settlement in the Promised Land, and after the building of the temple. Only to Moses and to the new worshipping community which developed as a result of the covenant through Moses was the personal name YHWH revealed. This was the same worshipping community that was struggling during the exile to recover its roots; it is no wonder therefore that all its reforms of whatever period are set in the context of the Mosaic covenant. Laws and regulations may be enlarged or added, but they are all in the interest of making a holy people for the most holy God who has called them to be his people. This is their supreme vocation.

SUGGESTIONS FOR STUDY AND DISCUSSION

1. What light does the Pentateuch throw on the cloud in the New Testament (Luke 9:34; Acts 1:9; 1 Thessalonians 4:17)?

2. What is the significance of priestly vestments worn today?

3. How would you respond to some one who said that if the numbers in the Bible are not accurate, there's no reason why we should believe any of it?

CHAPTER 9

Leviticus: Cult and Covenant

Passages for study: Leviticus; Ezekiel 43:1–5;
47:1–12; Isaiah 53; 62–63

Leviticus is a well-organized book, easily summarized as follows:

1. *Chapters 1–7. Laws governing sacrifice*
2. *Chapters 8–10. Institution of the priesthood*
3. *Chapters 11–16. Uncleanness and its treatment, i.e. occasions for sacrifice*
4. *Chapters 17–26. Instructions for practical holiness, sometimes known as the holiness code*
5. *Chapter 27. Appendix: vows and tithes.*

The name Leviticus in our English Bible comes from the Greek version and recognizes its close association with the Levites, the servants of the temple. The book is mainly concerned with worship and cult practices which are now largely obsolete. So at first sight it seems unnecessary to study it. Sacrifices are out-of-date any way, and the whole idea of animal sacrifice is abhorrent to nicely brought-up Westerners who are wealthy enough to eat meat frequently and to keep the slaughter-houses well out of sight. Yet although its detailed study may well be left to the scholars, the ideas of sacrifice and holiness provide such powerful symbols throughout the Scriptures that we must explore them further.

SACRIFICE

The English word sacrifice is derived from two Latin words meaning 'making', and 'holy'. The Hebrew equivalent is _corban,_ offering. Basically, therefore, a sacrifice is something offered to God. Leviticus makes it clear that for the Jews the sacrifice must be personal, and it must involve some cost to the giver. The animal, be it goat or bull, must be from the flock of the one who makes the offering; it would therefore have been a possible source of nourishment or profit, which is given up to God. The laying on of hands which was an essential preliminary, was a guarantee that the gift was a personal one (Leviticus 1:2; 3:1–2; etc.). Notice that the one who brought the gift also killed the animal. The blood was poured out, and was dealt with by the priest. For blood is powerful; it is the life.

> The life of the flesh is in the blood; and I have given it for you upon the altar to make atonement for your souls; for blood makes expiation by reason of the life that is within it.
>
> Leviticus 17:10–11

The way in which the blood was used varied with different types of sacrifice. In the whole burnt offering, the *holocaust* in Greek, the blood was thrown against the altar before the offering was cut in pieces and completely burnt on the altar. The sacrifice was called in Hebrew *olah*, or going up. Did this refer to the offerer going up to the altar, or to the smoke going up to heaven? If the latter, was this how Cain knew that Abel's sacrifice was acceptable while his was not? We can only guess.

Another type of offering was the peace-offering, described in chapters 3, and 7:17. In this the victim is shared—God, the priest, and the people all having an appointed share. This is the common sacrifice at festivals, and is accompanied with great rejoicing. In a part of South India where some Hindus still practise animal sacrifice, small family groups can be seen on the roads at the time of the festival, converging on the shrine. A goat or lamb is led at the head of each little procession; while women and babies travel in an ox-cart, men and older children follow on foot. The next day the processions return—with the carcase of the goat tied to the outside of the cart. The priests have had their share, and the entrails have been burnt, going up in smoke to Siva; the rest will be enjoyed by the family, probably the only meat they will eat until the next festival. The purpose of this sacrifice is clearly communion, between the god and the people, and with each other.

A third type of sacrifice was that of expiation, in Hebrew, *hattah*. The instructions for two varieties of this type of sacrifice, the sin offering and the guilt-offering, given in chapters 4 and 5:1–13, do not distinguish clearly between them; ancient traditions seem to have been combined. Most of the sins for which a sin-offering was prescribed were unconscious infringements of the ritual laws. One is reminded that Job offered such sacrifices lest his children should unconsciously have sinned (Job 1:5). The priests of the Exile were intent on producing a community wholly acceptable to God, and even unwitting sins must be expiated. The only deliberate offence which merited a sin offering was keeping silence when asked to witness under oath. (So Jesus was compelled to speak when Caiaphas asked him, 'Are you the Christ?' in Mark 14:60–62.) The blood in a sin-offering was shed near the altar, and some of it was smeared on to the 'horns', the most sacred part of the altar. The horns were four excrescences, one at each corner, and probably were some vestigial relic of ancient altars where Baal was featured on the horns of a bull.

As a sign that the sin was taken away the offender had no share in eating the victim. If the offence was that of the priest or of the whole congregation the animal offered was taken outside the camp, after the ritual slaughtering and special treatment of the blood, and there burnt, a visible sign that the sin had indeed been expiated, i.e. taken away.

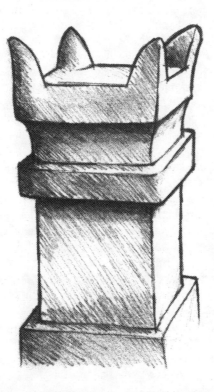

14. Sketch of altar found at Megiddo showing 'horns'

RESTORATION OF THE COVENANT RELATIONSHIP

Whatever may have been the motives of primitive sacrifices, or of those who brought the offerings, there is no trace in Leviticus of the notion that sacrifice was offered to appease the anger of God or to alter his will. Rather it was the means through which God met his people. Israel had broken the covenant, and had lost the special relationship with God which it had brought into being. But God had not changed, and the purpose of sacrifices in the thought of the writers of Leviticus was to restore this relationship—to make at-one-ment (Leviticus 1:4; 4:20). This is why the compilers were so careful to set the whole book in the context of the covenant. In the Hebrew Scriptures it is called by its opening words, 'And he said.' Thus it is continuous with the Book of Exodus, the book which describes the making of the covenant.

THE PURPOSE OF LEVITICUS

Exodus ends with the Lord in the tent of meeting, speaking to Moses; Leviticus begins in the same place. So the book is a continuation of the instructions for worship given at the end of Exodus. We saw in the last chapter that there was more in these instructions than could have been written by Moses in the tent of meeting, and that they were more likely to be a handbook prepared by those in exile for the right conduct of worship on their return. This suggestion seems more probable in the light of the orderly arrangement of Leviticus. The first chapters describing types of sacrifice are of general concern; the next are about the part played by the priests, and include ceremonies for their appointment. The ritual for the anointing of Aaron and of his sons is not described until chapter 8, after Moses had been instructed to assemble all the congregation at the door of the tent of meeting. This seems to have been the passage which originally followed the closing verses of Exodus, and it is a reasonable assumption that the earlier chapters, 1–7, were placed in this position later, though not necessarily written later. As in the other books of Pentateuch, there are evidences of older material elsewhere in Leviticus. The priests after the exile were longing to make a community fit for their holy calling as the people of God when restoration should become possible. Many of the rules may have been ancient and may have dated from the first temple, that of Solomon; others may have been in force only in the temple rebuilt under Zerubbabel.

THE DAY OF ATONEMENT

Before Judah could be accepted as God's people, there had to be some recognition of their failure in the past. A new fast was instituted, that of *Yom Kippur*, whose sacrificial ritual is described in chapter 16. First Aaron offered a bull to make expiation for himself and his family. Next two goats were brought; one was a sin-offering for all the people, the other was led out into the wilderness, bearing the sins of the whole people. The identity of Azazel remains a mystery, but the idea of a scapegoat fills a deep human need! After the instructions for the sacrifices in verses 29f. comes the command which Jews observe to this day, to keep a day of solemn mourning for their sins that they may again be worthy of the covenant.

RITUAL PURITY AND HOLINESS

The ritual for the Day of Atonement is nicely placed between two sections dealing with the necessary conditions for being the people of God. The first, in chapters 11–16, concerns ritual purity, and the second, in chapters 17–26 concerns holiness. This latter section is sometimes known as the holiness code, and most scholars think that it once had an independent existence. Cleanness and holiness are closely related in ancient thought. In English, the words holiness, health, and wholeness all stem from the same root; so, from a different source, do sanity, sanitation and sanctity. There is not the same connection in Hebrew, where the underlying belief seems to have been that unclean-ness was a mysterious force, which affected whatever came into contact with it. So those in contact with anything unclean themselves became 'untouchable', and needed ritual purification. Many taboos grew up in consequence. Some of these taboos were clearly concerned with what we today would call health, like the laws for the treatment of skin diseases. In passing, it should be noted that the leprosy common in the east is a different disease from that known today as leprosy. Some of the food taboos were also health precautions, as anyone who has seen pigs scavenging in semi-desert regions will appreciate; others are of unknown origin. Social anthropologists see in them some attempt at classifying the natural world, primitive man's attempt to gain mastery over his surroundings. Thus some animals are ruminants with cloven hooves; others are carnivores with clawed toes. What of those which fit into neither category? The unknown and the unusual are always causes of fear. So too is blood, the fear of which is apparent in other taboos, as well as in many ceremonies—from the priest's having to change his breeches after sprinkling the blood, to the rules for purification after childbirth. For all occasions of conscious contact with the unclean, specific rituals are laid down; for unconscious infringements by the whole community, the Day of Atonement makes provision.

THE HOLINESS CODE

After the cleansing comes the need to remain clean. Holiness is the condition of belonging to God. The holiness code is a collection of laws and rules from different periods, and those who wish to study them in detail should refer to the commentaries. Here we notice only that the first section deals with the slaughter of animals, which must always be regarded as a religious act because of the blood involved; this is followed by instructions about sexual conduct. In chapter 19 there is repeated refrain, 'Ye shall be holy, as I am holy.' The suggestion has been made that this was originally a liturgical response. The first four verses of the chapter are reminiscent of the Ten Commandments, particularly of those which distinguish the Jews from their neighbours, such as keeping the Sabbath and refraining from the use of images. These rules, although of ancient origin, would have been of particular importance in Babylon in order to maintain the separate identity of the Jews as the people of God. Other laws in this code date from different periods, but most of them have their counterpart in Exodus. All are concerned with practical matters of daily life, and one idea that comes across clearly is that every part of daily life comes under the care of God. As in Exodus, there is a marked concern for others, summarized in the verse which Jesus used when asked which was the greatest command-ment, 'Thou shalt love thy neighbour as thyself' (Leviticus 19:18; Mark 12:31). Jesus' interpretation of the Law was not original, as the whole verse indicates; his specific contribution was to live it out thoroughly, and to widen its implication to one's enemies!

The rest of the holiness code seems to be a jumble of miscellaneous rules. Some offences were punishable by death, and these are listed. So also are special instructions for priests, and for ensuring that holy gifts were kept holy, free from all contamination. Festivals and fasts are prescribed, as in the Book of Exodus, but with variations, the most noticeable of which is the mention of the Sabbath, which became a distinugishing mark of the Jews in exile. Amid details of rules for the regular service of the sanctuary, there is a curious example of case-law in which a foreigner is judged to be under the same condemnation as the Jews for blaspheming the name of God (24:10–23). The Sabbath became so important that what was probably originally a fallow year became known as the year of the Sabbath. Moreover every seventh Sabbath year, that is, every forty-ninth year, was to be a year of Jubilee. The Hebrew word translated Jubilee comes from the word for 'ram', and the year was ushered in by the blowing of the *shofar*, or ram's horn. Was the year of Jubilee ever a practicality, or was it just a dream of the priests, like the fertile valley of Ezekiel's vision? During this year every man was to go to his own home, and property reverted to its original owner. So the purpose of the regulations seems to have been the control of property. For the poor there were special provisions; a redeemer, a *go'el*, a member of his family, had to step in and purchase the land so that it did not pass to a foreigner. Not only must the poor relation be cared for, but the heritage of the land must be safeguarded.

The holiness code ends in chapter 26 with a summary of rewards and punishments. The reward for following the commandments of God is a time of fruitfulness and peace. 'I will again be your God.' Disobedience however, will bring a succession of disasters, as indeed it had done all through the history of the Jews. There are in this passage relics of ancient blessing and cursing ceremonies, but as it now stands it is a call to the Jews to choose. Renewal is possible, because God does not fail. He is the God who brought them out of the land of Egypt. He is YHWH.

The last chapter of Leviticus, coming after such a dramatic conclusion to the holiness code, is an appendix of unrelated matters which seem to have had no place elsewhere. Nevertheless, the tenor of the book is maintained, that the holy God of Israel accepts Israel as his people; but their response must be holiness in every detail of their lives.

FOR STUDY AND DISCUSSION

1. What does Paul mean by calling the death of Jesus a sacrifice? As the word 'sacrifice' has been so debased in modern speech, is it still sensible to apply it in this way? Can you suggest another?
2. Does your study of Leviticus throw light on these New Testament passages?

  a. Paul's request to the Romans, to be 'a living sacrifice, holy and acceptable to God' (Romans 12:1)

  b. 'Without the shedding of blood there is no forgiveness of sins' (Hebrews 9:22)

  c. 'Without the camp' (Hebrews 13:11–13).

3. What details of our daily life are not yet brought under the law of God? Or, to put the same question in other terms, does our righteousness exceed that of the scribes and Pharisees?

---CHAPTER 10---

On to the Promised Land

Passages for study: Numbers; Jeremiah 24–26;
Ezekiel 37:15f.; Obadiah 10–14; Haggai 2:10–14

THE BLESSING OF LAND IN WHICH TO DWELL

The best-known story in Numbers is that of the ass who spoke, and stopped Balaam in his tracks. The story is told at length in Numbers 22–24. Balak, king of Moab, was so scared of the approaching Israelites that he tried to make use of occult powers, engaging Balaam to pronounce a solemn curse upon them. Three times the ass tried to stop Balaam, until he promised to speak only as the Lord commanded him—a command which had previously been made the condition of his travelling (22:20)! Three times Balak provided material for sacrifice and demanded an oracle, each time paying the necessary fee. Each time instead of the curse he had asked for, he heard Balaam utter a blessing at the Lord's command. Another three-fold blessing was added to the story for good measure!

These blessings mark the climax of the book of Numbers in which the last part of God's promise to Abraham—that of land in which to dwell—nears its conclusion. The chapters following the Balaam story contain various regulations for rituals and items of legislation, mainly concerned with the occupation of the land. The book ends with the people camped near Jericho, poised to enter the land, brought there by the power of God in spite of all their difficulties and grumblings in the wilderness. Numbers is not, however, a straightforward account of their journey. It appears to be such a muddle that some commentators have given up hope of finding a pattern in it, describing it as a rag-bag of bits and pieces that would fit in nowhere else. This is to underestimate the compilers, who, however much they may have used ancient material, have, by the end, told how Moses, under God, brought the Israelites from Sinai to Jericho, and have so told their story that they give guidance to their readers in their own progress towards the fulfilment of their hopes.

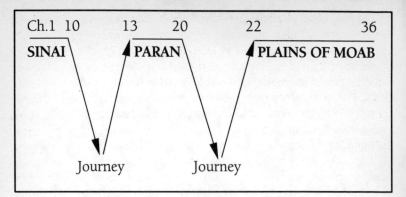

15. Diagram to show pattern of Numbers

STRUCTURE OF THE BOOK

The book begins where Leviticus left off, on Sinai, thus showing it to be part of the whole Torah, part of God's plan for his people. There are three locations for the stories that are recounted, Sinai, Paran and the Plains of Moab—where the book ends. Each area is a wilderness. In the wilderness of Paran there is the large oasis of Kadesh-Barnea where J and E locate their incidents, while P prefers to speak of Paran—perhaps reminding readers of the Hebrew title of the book, 'In the wilderness'. This is derived, not as is customary, from its first words, but from the fourth significant Hebrew word. Between each location mentioned is a description of journeying, and usually a regulation of some sort. There is thus a three-fold pattern in the book.

TRADITIONAL MATERIAL

In the central section the compilers have drawn largely on the traditional writings of J and E and a glance at chapter 21 will show the reason for the notion of a rag-bag. The chapter includes not only descriptions of three battles on the way, and the curious tale of the healing serpent; it also contains three songs. The first one seems to be a rhyme which defines the boundaries between tribes, the next is the song of the well, which was probably sung when a well was made, and repeated as a thanksgiving for God's provision of water. The third song is a triumph song of the Amorites over their own previous enemies. The Israelite victories over Og, king of Bashan, and Sihon, king of the

Amorites, were obviously such a tremendous boost to morale after forty years' wandering that they are mentioned frequently in the Scriptures. See Psalms 44:2; 135:10–12; 136:17f; also Amos 2:9; Nehemiah 9:22. One account of the battle gives the size of Og's bed as nine cubits in length and four in breadth (Deuteronomy 3:11). (A cubit is the length of a man's arm from the tip of his finger to his elbow, about 18 inches.) When the Israelites defeated the Amorites they would have enjoyed taunting their conquered foes with their own victory song! One of these songs, and possibly another, comes from the otherwise unknown 'Book of the Wars of the Lord'—evidence that the compilers were not relying on spoken tradition alone. When the whole chapter is recognized as a compilation of ancient traditions, and is viewed not simply as a move between two camping sites, but as part of the total pilgrimage, the 'odds and ends' element assumes a less important place. It cannot be removed entirely, however, since there is some overlapping with the wilderness stories in Exodus. Compare for example, Exodus 17 and Numbers 20:2–13. The same stories seem to have been used, though perhaps with a different emphasis, and possibly, even to make another 'three'.

THE AUTHORITY OF MOSES

The Lord is the initiator throughout, with Moses as his mediator. Notice the opening words, 'The Lord spoke to Moses', and the closing summary, 'These are the commandments and the ordinances which the Lord commanded by Moses to the people of Israel in the plains of Moab by the Jordan at Jericho.' In spite of much priestly material, including regulations for worship, Moses, not Aaron, is the key-figure. Even the Aaronic blessing, familiar to us today, was transmitted through Moses.

The Lord said to Moses, 'Say to Aaron and his sons, Thus shall you bless the people of Israel: you shall say to them,

'The Lord bless you and keep you:
The Lord make his face to shine upon you,
and be gracious unto you:
The Lord lift up his countenance upon you,
and give you peace.'

Numbers 6:22f

The question of authority is raised more than once. One tale, in chapter 16, tells of the revolt of Korah, aided and abetted by two sons of Reuben and others, against the authority of Moses and Aaron. (Some commentators think that two separate revolts have been confused in the telling.) Their complaint was that Moses and Aaron took too much upon themselves. 'All the congregation are holy, everyone of them, and the Lord is among them; why then do you exalt yourself above the assembly of the Lord?' When the earth opened up to receive the rebels, the judgment of God seemed clear to the onlookers. In such a way did some see the fire in York Minster in 1986! Later we are told that even Miriam questioned Moses' authority and she was smitten with leprosy. Aaron was equally guilty, and begged Moses to pray for her healing (12:1–16). The whole tale is an occasion for an oracular utterance in praise of Moses, declaring him to be greater than any prophet.

> If there is a prophet among you, I, Yahweh, make
> myself known to him in a vision,
> I speak with him in a dream.
> Not so with my servant Moses; he is entrusted with
> all my house.
> With him I speak clearly, and not in dark speech;
> and he beholds the form of the Lord

WHEN WAS IT COMPILED?

It seems that the writers felt a great need to stress the importance of Moses. Were they writing at a time when both Moses and the covenant needed stressing, perhaps in circumstances which led even to doubt of God's sovereignty? We have already seen that the final compilation was some time after the exile; how long after, we can only guess. Sacrifice was no longer possible; it is noteworthy that in Numbers offences are usually forgiven not by ritual act but as a result of Moses' intercession. From the contents of Numbers it seems that the exiles were so comfortably settled in Babylon that they were in danger of losing their identity. They were urged to remain distinct from their neighbours, distinguished by clothing as well as by their ways of worship and their observances. They were told to wear on their garments a fringe with a blue thread. Blue was the colour of holiness, featuring also on Aaron's turban (15:37–41; cf. Exodus 28:37). Still today such tassels are worn by Jews at the corners of their prayer-shawls. The census in the opening chapter of the book served as a reminder of their distinctive position as descendants of Israel and heirs of the promise. (It is this census, and another at the end, with their incredible numbers that gave rise to the Greek title, *Arithmoi*, literally translated into English—Numbers.) Whatever their circumstances may have been, the compilers were urgently calling the people back to an observance of the command-ments, that is, to the authority of Moses, through whom these had been given as the will of the Lord, their God.

Keeping the Sabbath free from work was the commandment which more than any other marked them out from their neighbours; it thus helped to give them a sense of community as well as being a reminder of their heritage. So the punishment for its neglect was especially severe. Hence the story of the man who was stoned to death because he picked up sticks on the Sabbath (15:32–36). When the Jews were once more back in their homeland the primacy of Sabbath observance was a matter of debate. This is clear from the question the lawyer put to Jesus, 'Which is the great commandment in the law?' Jesus did not answer as many scribes would have done, by quoting Numbers, 'Strict obser-vance of the Sabbath.' In a different context a different emphasis was needed. Jesus' answer was still from the Torah, and in Mark's version of the story we are told that the scribe approved of it:

> The first is, 'Hear, O Israel, Yahweh, our God, Yahweh is one; and you shall love Yahweh your God with all your heart and with all your soul and with all your mind.' And a second is like it, 'You shall love your neighbour as yourself.' On these two commandments depend all the law and the prophets.

> *Matthew 22:35ff.; quoting Deuteronomy 6:1f. and Leviticus 19:18*

Like Leviticus, every ordinance in Numbers is described as the word of the Lord given to Moses. It is an attempt to bring back the people to their vocation as people of the covenant. Although there is no mention of a possible return, the book ends on a note of promise, with the Promised Land in sight.

THE PRIESTLY CONTRIBUTION

The book had begun on Sinai, where God made known his presence to Moses. The opening chapters, which are from the priestly tradition, give an account of the camp on Sinai which is impossible to believe literally, but which nevertheless contains valuable insights. We have already considered, when discussing the priestly view of history in chapter 8, the impossibility of believing the vast numbers of men of military age. These numbers are given in detail, tribe by tribe (1:1–46). Thus the value of the peoples' heritage is emphasized, together with the importance of the community as a whole, in which every single tribe had a part. In Exodus men and women brought gifts for the tabernacle 'as their hearts were stirred'; in Numbers each tribe brought for its transport an equal share, a wagon for every two of the princes and an ox for each. Each tribe also brought an identical oblation (Exodus 35:21f; Numbers 7:2f). As the Levites were set apart for service in the tabernacle, they were not included in the first census, but were numbered separately (1:47–54; 3:14f.).

The furnishings of the tabernacle, as in Exodus, are more reminiscent of the Chroniclers' account of Solomon's temple than descriptive of what would be suitable for a portable tent in the desert. The compilers may have sensed this, for they give detailed instructions for disman-tling it and for carrying it, each branch of the tribe of Levi having a special task (ch. 4). But even the Levites were not allowed to look on the most holy things. They were not allowed into the most holy place, and, before moving camp, the sacred vessels were to be covered with veils by the priests lest the Levites who were concerned with their transport should look on them and die. The camp was kept holy by the exclusion of lepers, of those who had any kind of discharge, and of those who had been in contact with the dead (5:1).

Again as in Exodus, the tabernacle differed from the tent of meeting in its position in the very centre of the camp. Here is the priestly way of symbolizing the presence of God in the midst of his people. According to Numbers the tabernacle occupied the symbolic position of the king's tent, surrounded on all sides by those of his troops, each troop having its own battle standard. When the camp set out on its journey, that is, when the cloud rose up from the tabernacle, the ark of God went with them, for it was from between the cherubim above the ark that Moses had heard the voice of the Lord (7:89). We know that the ark was taken in to battle after the settlement, when the Philistines were a threat (1 Samuel 4:3). It was during the settlement that Israel had become a militant people, calling God, he Lord of hosts', a title not used in the Pentateuch (1 Samuel 17:45). It seems likely that the compilers of Numbers were reading back a later practice when they ascribed to Moses the battle-cry as the ark was taken in procession, 'Arise, O Lord, and let thine enemies be scattered' (10:35; cf. Psalm 68:1–2). Later in the book when an abortive attempt was made to enter the Promised

Land, the compilers tell us it was because the ark was not with them, for to them the ark indicated the presence of God (14:43–45).

Even in this first section there are a few 'odds and ends', apparently unrelated items. Consider, for example, the trial by ordeal of the woman taken in adultery, instructions for the Nazirite vow, and the making of the silver trumpets which were to rally the people for worship or for battle (5:11–end; 6:1–21; 10:1–10). There is also an account of a second Passover feast on Sinai—presumably because Moses took so long to deliver all these instructions! This account, however, provides the opportunity for a scrap of legislation about those unfortunate enough to miss the Passover because of temporary uncleanness. More 'odds and ends' of ritual occur in the course of the book. Chapter 15, for example, contains instructions for sacrifice and celebration reminiscent of the rules in Leviticus. These would have been impossible when the book was being written, but the compilers had their vision firmly on the end of the journey. The phrase, 'when you come into the land', is repeated (2, 18). Restoration after the exile was the hope of Israel. The book is not a detailed history, but guidance for the present, based on past experience.

ADDITIONAL POINTS TO NOTICE

A few other items on the journey invite comment for various reasons. The ambiguous serpent of Genesis 3 appears again. One occasion of grumbling coincided with a plague of serpents whose bite was cured by Moses lifting up the brazen serpent. Hundreds of years later, a brazen serpent in the temple was removed during Hezekiah's reform; it had obviously become an object of worship (21:f.; 2 Kings. 18:4). As a symbol of healing the serpent needs interpreting in the light of a comment in Wisdom. 'He who turned towards it was saved, not by what he saw, but by Thee, the Saviour of all' (Wisdom 16:7).

A point of current relevance is the distrust between Edom and Israel. The king of Edom refused the Israelites passage through his territory in spite of their promise to keep to the highway—an old enmity which was exacerbated at the time of the exile. We can only guess what unbrotherly actions lay behind Obadiah's outburst, but there is no doubt of the ill-feeling. Any peace talks today need to take account of this ancient inherited prejudice!

Lastly, one of the oracles of Balaam has sometimes been interpreted as a forecast of the Messiah.

A star shall come forth out of Jacob,
and a sceptre shall arise out of Israel

Numbers 24:17

It may well be a later addition, but even if original, Balaam was not looking beyond the possession of the Promised Land as the mention of Moab shows, and certainly not beyond the exile. The star would have been associated by later readers with the star of David, as it was in the Dead Sea Scrolls.

For the Dead Sea Community, the star was the kingly Messiah, and 'the sceptre represents the leader of the community'. The leader of the last Jewish revolt against the Romans in AD135 changed his name from Bar Cozeba to Bar Cochba, 'son of the Star', in order to declare his messianic status.

The closing chapters of Numbers are again from the priestly writers, and look forward to the time of settlement in the land; there are in it more items of religious observance. For the priest, ritual was of paramount importance for maintaining the purity of God's chosen people. These rules mean little to us today, yet ritual of some sort plays a vital role in the lives of everyone of us. We are all creatures of habit and convention, and if one ritual ceases for any reason, another grows up in its place. When school uniform is given up new peer-group 'uniforms' take their place, be they jeans or multi-coloured hairstyles! Labour Day replaces May Day, and saints' day holidays, instituted to give respite to workers, become merely Bank Holidays. Whatever our personal routines may be, we obtain from them some feeling of security. This is part of the importance of ritual. Another, more important, part is the sense of community which it brings. With this comes another function of ritual—education. Through traditional nursery rhymes and stories children learn both the language and the ideas of their inheritance; similarly, through repeated acts of worship we learn to understand and to articulate something of the mystery of God. There is always the danger that the ritual may be so blindly followed that it becomes important in its own right—an end in itself, rather than a means to an end. So, from time to time, prophetic voices are heard. Nourished by the ritual, they have penetrated beyond its acts and words, and have learnt for themselves something of the mystery of God. Listening to his voice, they have a message with which to recall others to him. Yet without any ritual to feed and educate the community, could the prophets ever have arisen? Both ritual and prophecy have their place.

Numbers ends with the Promised Land in sight. All seems complete, and yet there is one more book in the Torah. The prophetic interpretation of the Exodus is still to come.

SOME NEW TESTAMENT REFERENCES

The cloud
Luke 9:34; Acts 1:9; 1 Thessalonians 4:17

Silver Trumpets
Numbers 10:1–10; Joel 2:1; Matthew 24:31;
1 Thessalonians 4:16; 1 Corinthians 15:52

The Brazen Serpent
John 3:14

QUESTIONS FOR DISCUSSION

1. Is there any one commandment which needs emphasizing today more than the others?
2. What do you understand by 'the judgment of God'? Can justice and mercy be reconciled?
3. Discuss the value of the ritual to which you are accustomed.

CHAPTER 11

Deuteronomy I:
Its origin and structure

Passages for study: 2 Kings 17–23; Jeremiah 11:1–8;
Hosea 11:1ff; Amos 4:4–5; 5:1–5, 21–24

Of the making of many books there is no end, and much learning
is a weariness to the flesh.

These lines were written more than two thousand years ago. The writer, known as the Preacher or the Philosopher, according to which translation of the Bible is used, had found all worldly paths to happiness fruitless. The only way of finding satisfaction, he concluded, was to return to one's Creator.

This is the end of the matter: Fear God and keep his command-
ments; for this is the whole duty of man.
Ecclesiastes 12:12–13

THE CONTENT OF DEUTERONOMY

Deuteronomy is one of the 'many books' available to the Preacher, and was so well esteemed that it was included with the Priestly compilation of the Books of Moses to form the Torah, the Pentateuch. After the end of Numbers there seems little more to add; the promises have been fulfilled, the covenant made, and the land is in sight. What can Deuteronomy say that has not already been said?

At first sight, there seems little new in Deuteronomy. The first four chapters are a summary of journeyings in the wilderness said to be retold by Moses. The Ten Commandments re-appear in chapter 5; rules for tithing, and for festivals are repeated later in the book, and some of the case-law is the same as in earlier parts of the Torah. Many of the laws in the Book of the Covenant, i.e. Exodus 21–23, are repeated. The name 'Deuteronomy' means, in fact, 'Second Law' (from Greek: *deutero*, second, and *nomos*, law). Its Hebrew name, 'Words' comes, as is usual for a new scroll, from its first significant word. These 'words' in their totality are set in the form of a final exhortation before Moses' death, which is described in the last chapter.

Amid the exhortations are indications that the book was written long after Moses had died. There are instructions that the king should have a written copy of the law, and read it diligently (17:18f); yet there was no king appointed before Saul, some two hundred years after Moses. Laws about olive trees and vineyards do not belong to a desert community; nor did such a community build houses, or have a cash economy (24:20f; 22:8; 23:19f). The clearest sign of a late date comes in chapter 12, with the demand for one central place of worship and the destruction of all others—'the place which the Lord shall choose'. This chapter corresponds very closely with the account of Josiah's reforms related in 2 Kings 22 and 23, and it has for long been accepted that the central part of Deuteronomy was the Law book discovered during the cleansing of the temple ordered by Josiah. Some part of the book therefore probably dates from the time just before Josiah's reforms, about 621BC. *(re. the reforms = 621 BC p.103)*

There is much teaching, however, about the conduct of the holy war which seems to belong to the times of the Judges and Saul rather than to a more settled area. The nations whom the Lord would deliver to the advancing Israelites were to be utterly destroyed (Deuteronomy 7:1f).

It was failure to observe this rule which resulted in the inability of Joshua to capture Ai until Achan's disobedience had been discovered (Joshua 7). Saul also failed when in fighting the Amalekites, he refused to kill their king, Agag, intending instead to parade him victoriously before the crowds. His disobedience is given as the cause of his failure as king (1 Samuel 15).

All wars were to be conducted in the name of the Lord. Yet there are puzzles. Many classes were to be excused from active service, for example, those who were afraid, those who had recently planted a vineyard, or married a wife (Deuteronomy 20:1f). Fruit trees were not to be cut down. Women prisoners were not to be raped, but rather treated with such respect that if a man desired one, he was to make her his wife—but only after she had been allowed a due period of mourning (Deuteronomy 20:1–9; 21:10–15). These provisions seem hardly to apply to a period when the invading Israelites were fighting for possession of a new territory. Are they a later adaptation of the Law? Are they a re-writing of the rules applicable to Josiah's newly recruited army, necessary because of the withdrawal of Assyrian troops? Some of us today may find the sacrifice of everything and everyone in the city a repellent idea, but napalm and scorched earth, even bombing of entire cities seem to be a recognized necessity of modern warfare! There is no doubt that much of the Deuteronomic ideal of war is more humane than ours—for the Israelites at least! Were the compassionate instructions in Deuteronomy about exemptions from fighting contemporary with those to devote all cattle and humans to God by destroying them, or were they a later ideal? Certainly Deuteronomy is as much a compilation of ancient tradition and later re-interpretation as the other books of the Pentateuch! Compiling the whole book as a sermon of Moses is a literary device similar to that we found in Leviticus and Numbers, ensuring that readers of the book understand that its contents belong to the covenant.

VARYING APPLICATIONS OF THE LAWS

Is it possible to posit a particular situation for the final compilation of the book? By discovering the context in which it was written we should be better able to understand its message, and so to translate it into our own context. Every age has its own particular needs. The word of God is eternal, and each generation hears that part of it which befits its own situation. Since the Book of Leviticus may have been drawn up for a community returning from exile, its rules for sacrifices therefore have no meaning for us today, but the underlying idea of holiness remains constant, and must be interpreted in terms our generation can understand. So it is with Deuteronomy. The United Nations Organization would be hard put to it to apply exactly the Deuteronomic rules for a holy war, indeed, it is doubtful whether in the present accumulation of weapons of destruction there can ever be such a thing as a holy war. Yet the underlying principles in Deuteronomy need to be understood—and applied! Their basis is compassion.

The way in which a law develops to fit a different context may be seen by comparing Exodus 23:10f. with Deuteronomy 15:1. Even by the time the Exodus passage was written down, possibly in the time of Elijah and Elisha, a settled agricultural community had been established. In Deuteronomy the same law of release is stated, and then, in verses 2, applied to a money economy. The next verses in the form of an exhortation, are typical of much of the central section of Deuteronomy.

COVENANT RENEWAL

One small word occurs with remarkable frequency throughout Deuteronomy, the word *today*. All occasions of its use are related to the covenant, viz., 8:18; 11:26; 11:32; 26:17f. There are definite

X Ex. = leave land fallow every 7th yr.
Deut. = forgo all money owed to you.

instructions for reading the law at the Feast of Tabernacles during the year of release (Deuteronomy 31:9–13). Joshua 24 describes such a gathering for covenant renewal, and we know that Elkanah was accustomed to visit the shrine at Shiloh for an annual feast (1 Samuel 1:3–4). Was this an occasion for the renewal of the covenant? Was Deuteronomy compiled for just such an occasion? The words at the beginning of chapter 5 are indications of a much later celebration of the covenant than would have been possible for Moses; they are words still used in the annual celebration of the Passover today.

The Lord our God made a covenant with us in Horeb. The Lord made not this covenant with our fathers, but with us, even with us, who are all of alive today.

The prophets of the eighth century BC whose words have been preserved for us were conscious of their peoples' failure to keep the covenant. Micah's oracles in the name of Yahweh address Israel as 'My people' (Micah 3:5; 6:3–5). This is the keynote also of the whole of Hosea's oracles. Amos declared, 'You only have I known of all the peoples of the earth' (Amos 3:2). This was the time when the power of Assyria was increasing. The prophets' warnings went unheeded and in 721BC the northern tribes were conquered by Assyria. Although the eighth-century prophets were the first whose oracles were written down, they were the successors of a long tradition in the north. Many prophets including Elijah and Elisha, had inveighed against the worship of Canaanite Baalim and other foreign deities. It seems more than likely that some of the followers of this prophetic 'school' should, when disaster finally came, flee across the border into Judah, the only remaining tribe. They would have taken with them not only the records of Amos and Hosea, and their ancient traditions, but also their fear that the entire covenant community should disappear. They may also have inspired Hezekiah's short-lived reforms. The Assyrian armies came to the very gates of Jerusalem. Assyria gained complete domination on Hezekiah's death, reinforcing the fear of the destruction of the entire community. Followers of Yahweh seem to have gone under cover. Here *Part* is a likely situation for the origin of the hidden book. By the time Josiah *DEUT* came to the throne, Assyrian power was weakening, and when he was eighteen he began to remove its influence from the temple. In the year 621BC his reforms were accelerated and extended by the discovery of the hidden book, and its authentication by the prophetess Huldah.

The people's worst fears were realized soon after. In 597 the Babylonians, who were now masters in Mesopotamia, took into exile the cream of the Jerusalem population. Eleven years later the city was destroyed. Jeremiah was active during this time, and his prophecies of disaster if the people did not repent led him into conflict with the king and his ministers. Jeremiah was supported by Shaphan and Baruch, who are called 'scribes'. We first hear of scribes in the time of Hezekiah, and they are closely connected with the prophets. Were these the same class of people who had brought the message of Amos and Hosea to Judah and who wrote the law book discovered by Shaphan, who was also a scribe? Was it their followers who completed Deuteronomy during the exile? Were there other traditions brought from the north at the time of its fall? These are all questions as yet unresolved.

The covenant between God and Israel seems to have been set in the form of a covenant or treaty such as has been known between nations from Hittite archives dating from about the thirteenth century BC. It was probably the common form of agreement between any two parties, like the treaty between Solomon and Hiram, king of Tyre (1 Kings 5:1–12). The major sections of such treaty form seem to be as follows:

1. Preamble
   This usually took the form of a declaration about the king or power who was making the treaty.
2. Historical prelude
   The occasion for the treaty, often a résumé of the benevolent deeds of the great power.
3. The requirement of the treaty
   Stipulations and commands.
4. Provision for preservation of the document
5. Witnesses to the treaty
6. Blessings and curses
   The one making the covenant promised assistance to those who kept it, but declared disaster on those who violated it.

It is clear that many of these elements are present in Deuteronomy, and using this as a guide, it is possible to work out a summary of the whole book. Leaving on one side for the moment most of the first four chapters, there is a summary from 4:44 onwards of the journeys in the wilderness when Moses first gave the law; here is the historical prelude. The next two chapters repeat the commandments given when the covenant was first made, adding an exhortation and an interpretation. Apart from a brief historical interlude from 9:8 to 10:11 exhortations continue until chapter 12, and include a mention of blessings and curses at the end of chapter 8. Chapters 12 to 26 form another legal section, with laws both ancient and 'modern', many of them applying the commandments to everyday living. Then come two chapters of blessings and curses. The first of these, 27, seems to be an insertion from another source, and includes what is apparently a liturgical recital of specific cursing (which is used in the 1662 Book of Common Prayer in the Commination Service). Chapter 28 is the conclusion to the covenant, followed by an exhortation on faithfulness to the covenant. This basic outlines suggests that the editors were emphasizing in the structure of their final work the importance of the covenant whose memory was kept alive at an annual celebration. Yet such an outline does not fit the covenant pattern exactly, as the following summary shows.

CONTENTS AND STRUCTURE OF DEUTERONOMY

A 1:1—4:43 **First discourse**
            1:1–5 Introduction
            1:6–29 Looking back on history
            4:1–40 Exhortations
            4:41–43 Cities of refuge
B 4:44—11 **The basic covenant**
            4:4—49 Introduction: historical setting
            5—9:8 The Divine Law, with exhortations
            9:8—10:11 Historical section
            10:12—11:32 More exhortation
C 12–26 **Central legal section**
            Laws of Josiah's reformation and earlier, with teaching
D 27–28 **Blessings and curses**
E 29–30 **Moses' third sermon, insisting on covenant demands**
F 31–34 **Various appendices**
            31:1–8 Moses' last instructions
            31:9–13 Instructions to Levites for ceremony of
              covenant renewal
            31:14–15, 23 Commissioning of Joshua
            32:1–44 Song of Moses, with introduction
              in 31:16–22, 24–30
            33 Moses' blessing
            34 Death of Moses.

The central legal section, followed by blessings and curses seem to belong to a treaty pattern, and there is a very long preamble! Assuming the original preamble begins with 4:44, the main body of the book could well be a formula for a service of the renewal of the covenant. If this theory is accepted the opening chapters may be regarded as additions, as the last undoubtedly are, from different periods. The answer to this puzzle is generally agreed to be that Deuteronomy is only the first of several books compiled by the same group of men and perhaps their followers, known to scholars as 'the Deuteronomists', or the Deuteronomic School.

The Deuteronomists not only compiled a book of the Law in the light of the new understanding gained through the prophets, designed especially to fit the current political and international situation, they also wrote the history of the whole covenant community since the time of Moses. This is contained in the books known to the Jews as 'The Former Prophets', and include Joshua, Judges, Samuel and Kings. The first chapters of Deuteronomy form an introduction to the complete history, a summary of the history leading up to the covenant on Horeb. The covenant section proper is in no way a new Law, but a strong restatement of the same covenant which was described in Exodus. It has been suggested that the final three chapters should be regarded as the conclusion of the Pentateuch as a whole. Certainly the song in chapter 33 fits a period fairly soon after the settlement in the land, when all the tribes were still extant, and the command to 'destroy' was relevant. Was it perhaps a psalm to be sung in procession at a festival of covenant renewal at Shiloh?

To summarize, the book of Deuteronomy is both an introduction to the history of Israel which was completed only after the fall of Judah in 586BC, and written from the standpoint of the prophets, and also a restatement of the covenant in the context of a political disaster. Unless there were a return to the covenant, there could be no possibility of a return to the land, nor even the survival of the race. Although based on the same covenant, the outlook of Deuteronomy is different from that of Leviticus, and its understanding of the relation between God and his people is based, not as the priests saw it, on religious duties, but on the personal response which had led the prophets to their deeper knowledge of his love.

SUGGESTIONS FOR STUDY AND DISCUSSION

1. Find in the prophets references to the covenant, and to God's relationship with his people. Look again at Jeremiah 31:31–34.
2. What did the Deuteronomists mean by a holy war? Can there be such a thing today?
3. Try to write a modern version of the Ten Commandments, without obscuring their original meaning.

—— CHAPTER 12 ——

Deuteronomy II:
The message

Passages for study: Deuteronomy;
Jeremiah 7:1–10; 30–31; Hosea 1–3; Isaiah 46

RECALL TO THE COVENANT

Deuteronomy is based on the same traditions of the miraculous exodus from Egypt as the other books of the Pentateuch. It differs from them in establishing one central place of worship, and also in interpreting laws to suit changed circumstances. These differences alone do not seem sufficient to account for its appeal to those men and women in all ages who have ears to hear. Deuteronomy is imbued with the distilled wisdom of prophets who have not only studied the Law but have listened to the word of God speaking to them in their own situation.

For the writers of the Pentateuch, the three-fold promise to Abraham—of posterity, land and relationship with God—was sealed by the covenant on Sinai, or, according to E and to Deuteronomy, on Horeb. By the time that Deuteronomy was compiled, the Jews, the only surviving Israelites, were in imminent danger of extinction. The arrangement of the book is related to this danger, and to the conditions necessary for survival. First and foremost, it is a recall to the covenant. The second 'sermon' of Moses begins with a plea to Israel to give heed to the statutes and ordinances which he had taught them—and to '*Do* them, that you may live' (4:1). After many other earnest exhortations scattered throughout the chapter to remember God and to keep his commandments, there comes this final appeal for repentance to a people apparently already in exile, and again in danger of extinction.

> The Lord will scatter you among the peoples, and you will be left few in number among the nations where the Lord will drive you ... But from there you will seek the Lord, and you will find him, if you seek after him with all your heart and with all your soul. When you are in tribulation, and all these things come to pass in the latter

days, you will return to the Lord your God and obey his voice, for the Lord your God is a merciful God; he will not fail you or destroy you or forget the covenant with our fathers which he swore to them.

Deuteronomy 4:27ff.

RECALL TO OBEDIENCE

The call to obedience is repeated throughout the book in the starkest possible terms. The survival of the people of Israel would depend on their turning from other gods and following the commands of the Lord who had brought them out of the land of Egypt. Idolatry was the great sin. The choice was clear. Should the race die out, the people alone would be responsible, the choice was theirs.

See, I have set before you this day life and good, death and evil.
Deuteronomy 30:15f.

INDIVIDUAL RESPONSIBILITY

The promise of posterity to Abraham had been linked to his obedience. He had obeyed the call to leave his own country and to set out into the unknown. Each repetition in Genesis of the promise to him was linked with some act of obedience. His faith was reckoned to him for righteousness. So too for the exiles, the promise of posterity and of the continuance of the race depended on their obedience to the covenant, and could be forfeited by their faithlessness. The same idea occurs also in 8:19–20; 11:26–32; 29:24–28.

The people themselves would perish, being punished for their own sins, not for those of their ancestors. To them 'alive at that day' were the commandments given. 'I am he who brought you out of the land of Egypt ... Thou shalt have no other gods before me.' Often today the rider to the second commandment is misquoted, 'I am a jealous God visiting the iniquity of the fathers upon the children to the third and fourth generation.' To stop here is to imply a vindictive God without mercy. The sentence continues, 'of those who hate me, but showing steadfast love to thousands of those who love me and keep my commandments.' There is no punishment for those who turn from their wickedness. The Israelites had worshipped other gods for centuries; now away from their homeland they were reaping the reward of their infidelity. Yet God was still willing to save. The God who is to be served in the covenant is the God who has saved and who continues to save. God's will to punish is far outweighed by his will to save! The people themselves must choose whether to perish, or to return.

GOD'S CHOICE OF ISRAEL

Choice often figures in Deuteronomy. Not only were the people told to choose; God himself had chosen Israel. This is stated in the summary of the covenant at the end of chapter 26.

> You have declared this day concerning the Lord that he is your God, and that you will walk in his ways and keep his command- ments... and the Lord has declared this day concerning you that you are a people for his own possession, as he has promised you... and that you shall be a people holy to the Lord your God.

26:17-end; see also 4:20, 37; 7:6-9

The importance of the covenant is reflected in the treaty form in which the main section of Deuteronomy is framed. The introduction to Moses' third 'sermon', in chapters 29 and 30, speaks of a second covenant in the land of Moab. The underlying treaty pattern, of historical setting, basic principle, and blessing and curse are all present, although the whole section seems a little confused. The treaty form, ending with blessings and curses, underlines Israel's failure, and so implies that the sufferings which culminated in the exile were a direct result of their apostasy.

DEALING WITH SUFFERING

Not all suffering, however, is the result of sin. There had been much suffering during the wilderness years. Has Deuteronomy anything to say about this apparently unmerited suffering of scarcity and weari- ness? There are two suggestions, which are not theoretical, but which give a guide to the way in which such suffering may be dealt with. First, it may be educational. 'As a man disciplines his son, so the Lord your God disciplines you' (8:5). Or it may be testing (8:2; cf. Exodus 16:6; 20:20). We sometimes use the word 'testing' as a synonym for 'temptation' which has overtones of enticement to evil. Yet even 'temptation' has its origin in making the object fit for the work it has to do. We speak of the 'tempering' of steel. The greater the weight of responsibility to be borne, the more stringent must be the testing, whether it be for a jumbo-jet or for a post in MI5. Would those whom God chose to be his holy people be worthy of their task? Secondly, there is the assurance that the Lord was always with his people, even in the wilderness. In the words of Moses' song:

> He found him in a desert land,
> and in the howling waste of the wilderness;
> he encircled him, he cared for him,
> he kept him as the apple of his eye.
> Like an eagle that stirs up its nest,
> that flutters over its young,
> spreading out its wings, catching them,
> bearing them on its pinions,
> the Lord alone did lead him,
> and there was no foreign god with them.

Deuteronomy 32:10f.

THE PROMISE OF LAND

Exiled from what they had considered the land of promise, the Deuteronomists naturally spoke of a return, but their attitude to the land was not identical with that of the priestly writers who saw the land itself as holy. For the Deuteronomists it was the people who were holy; the land belonged to God. It too was apportioned by the choice of God. He gave Seir to Esau. (There is here none of the Israelites' pleading with the king of Edom to allow them passage which was in the account in Numbers.) Ammon was given to the sons of Lot (2:4; 2:19). That these verses are so confused that they make difficult reading does not affect the Deuteronomic idea that God gave the land to whomsoever he chose. 'Not because of your righteousness or the uprightness of your heart are you going in to possess their land, but because of the wickedness of these nations the Lord your God is driving them out before you' (9:5–6). And Israel's wickedness would in turn, result in their own removal from the land. This was not theirs by inalienable right; their possession of it depended on their observance of the covenant. With a return to God, they might again enjoy its privileges (4:26, 30; 6:3).

DANGERS OF TANGIBLE SYMBOLS

The frequent mention of idolatry raises an issue beyond that of worshipping other gods. Idols are material symbols of the deity, and however innocent a symbol may be in origin, it fills a deep human need, and may very soon be thought to be endowed with magical powers, and may even become an object of worship in itself. The history of religion abounds in such misapprehensions, from the black stone of Diana in Ephesus to the black Madonna in Chartres. For the priestly writers the tent of meeting had become the tabernacle, housing the ark whereon the Lord had his dwelling-place between the cherubim. The Deuteronomists insisted throughout their writing of Israel's history that Jeroboam's bulls had been at the root of the disaster which befell the northern kingdom. The people had made them into an object of worship instead of a symbol. Fearing the ark might similarly be worshipped, the Deuteronomists therefore put into the account of the building of Solomon's temple, which housed the ark, a solemn affirmation that God did not dwell therein.

> But will God indeed dwell on the earth? Behold, heaven and the highest heaven cannot contain thee; how much less this house which I have built! Yet have regard to the prayer of thy servant and to his supplication, O Lord my God ... that thy eyes may be open night and day towards this house, the place of which thou hast said, 'My name shall be there' ... when they pray toward this place, hear thou in heaven thy dwelling place; and when thou hearest, forgive.
>
> *1 Kings 8:27–30*

God's name was in the temple, it belonged to him. The same superstition that turns symbols into idols was still in the mind of the people when, before the exile, Jeremiah spoke to them. He warned against the uselessness of thinking that because they had the temple, wherein God's name dwelt, the people of Judah were safe from destruction even while breaking the laws of the covenant (Jeremiah 7:1–15). For Deuteronomy the ark is the symbol, not of God's presence, but of his covenant. It contained the stone tablets on which the commandments were written (Deuteronomy 10:1–5). It is never spoken of as the dwelling place of God. It was not to be taken into battle, as it had been when the Philistines captured it (1 Samuel 4–5). Instead, while conducting a holy war, the priest was given instructions to speak to the people reminding them that the Lord is with them. He 'walks in the midst of the camp' (20:2f.; 23:14). Notice in chapter 12 how 'the place which the Lord shall choose' is described (vv. 5, 11).

'I AM GOD AND NOT MAN'

In other ways too Deuteronomy avoids some of the anthropomorphic ideas of the earlier books. Compare, for example, Exodus 19:11, 20 with Deuteronomy 4:36. The elders 'saw' God in Exodus 24:9–11; the chief danger on the holy mountain was that the people might 'gaze upon God'. Such expressions do not occur in Deuteronomy. The people 'hear his voice' (4:3; 5:28). The prophets had come to know him directly by hearing his voice. It is true that when Isaiah describes his vision of the majesty of God he speaks of 'seeing' the Lord seated on a throne, and Amos 'saw' God standing before the altar (Isaiah 6:1; Amos 9:1). These are exceptions; usually for the prophets it is God's words that are all important. The danger is not in 'seeing' him, but in not attending to what he says. He is the one to whom 'belong heaven and the heaven of heavens, the earth and all that is in it'. What he requires of his chosen people is that they should 'fear him, to walk in his ways, and to love him' (10:12–14).

The basic issue is not one of keeping individual commandments, but of loyalty to God. The application of regulations might be altered to suit different circumstances—in moving from a semi-nomadic life to one of agriculture, from a primitive community to an economy involving lending money on usury, or from a time of prosperity to one of defeat. When at the beginning of the exile there was danger of the community losing its identity, the priests stressed the need for observing those commandments which distinguished them; thus in Numbers a man was put to death for picking up sticks on the Sabbath. The danger for the compilers of Deuteronomy was different, and they felt that nothing less than a total commitment to the whole covenant was necessary. So the simple statement in Exodus 22:20, 'Whoever sacrifices to any god, save to the Lord only, shall be put to death,' is enlarged and emphasized in chapter 13 of Deuteronomy. Any who led others to idolatry, whether they be false prophets or close friends and relatives, were to be punished by death (13:2, 6, 13). The general tenor of most regulations is amazingly humane; individuals are punished only when their offence is liable to harm the whole community.

THE DEVELOPMENT OF MONOTHEISM

In Exodus, the teaching was clear that there was one God for Israel, and the people were commanded to have no other gods 'before' Yahweh (Exodus 20:2). In a part of the world where each community felt under the protection of its own special deity, it is amazing that the Jews came to realize that there was but one God, creator and sustainer of the whole universe. The experience of the exile, was the 'eagle's stirring up the nest' which led the prophets of the time to this discovery. While some were feeling they could not sing the Lord's song in a strange land, Ezekiel, one of the first group of exiles, saw the 'heavens opened' and he heard the voice of God (Ezekiel 1–2). Deutero-Isaiah learnt that the gods of Babylon were not all-powerful, and he poured scorn on those who bought gold and hired a goldsmith to make an object of worship. He declared the monotheistic faith which Judaism has given to the world.

> *Thus says the Lord, the King of Israel,*
> *and his Redeemer, the Lord of hosts,*
> *I am the first, and I am the last;*
> *beside me there is no god.*

Isaiah 44:6

Whenever Jews today meet together for worship, they recite the verses from Deuteronomy 6:4 known as the *Shema*,

> **Hear, O Israel, the Lord our God is one Lord; and you shall love the Lord your God with all your heart, and with all your soul, and with all your strength.**

The first half of the Shema consists of only four Hebrew words, and there is more than one way of translating them. Perhaps the earliest version was a call to avoid the worship of the Baalim when the people arrived in Canaan, Yahweh is our God, Yahweh alone. The verse may however be read as a statement of monotheism, Yahweh, our God, is one Yahweh. There are other possibilities also. Thus, 'Yahweh, our God, is to be the only one whom the Israelites worship', or Yahweh, our God is the sole God. Whichever meaning is accepted, he is to be loved completely!

114

HOW CAN WE LOVE GOD?

We need to be aware of the danger involved in the interpretation of the word 'love'. To the Deuteronomists neither it nor the word 'fear' have the emotional content we are apt to give them today. They are covenant words. Examples have been found in Assyrian documents showing that the term translated 'love' means undivided loyalty to one's overlord. To love God implies total commitment to him, complete dedication to the terms of the covenant. He is a 'jealous' God—zealous for his covenant, permitting no rival, no serving other gods. Here is the reason for the Pharisees' zeal for the minutest detail of the Law. According to Rabbinic teaching the covenant involves acceptance of the exclusive kingship of Yahweh. 'Yahweh is king' is the burden of many Psalms, as it is the theme of Samuel's reluctance to appoint an earthly king in 1 Samuel 8:7 and 10:19. Yet there is more to the word than mere adherence to the letter of the law. It includes heart and soul—perhaps conscience is more easily understood by moderns than soul. For the prophets it meant more than blind obedience to detailed regulations of a dictator; Hosea saw the relationship as that of a wife to her husband. Deuteronomy sees it rather as that of a son to his father. A child accepts what his father gives, and responds with trust. As with continued attentiveness and obedience a son grows in knowledge of his father, so God's children may learn to 'know' him. This was the vision of Jeremiah. 'They shall all know me, from the greatest to the least.'

GOD'S LOVE FOR US

The love of God to which man responds is far beyond the understanding of our finite minds. Some people find it first through his creation, some through human love. Still others discover when they fall that, 'Underneath are the everlasting arms' (33:27). Yahweh, the God who is, and who will be, is the Creator of all that is—and its redeemer. Small wonder that Deuteronomy tells us to keep his words on our heart, and to teach them diligently to our children. In the words ascribed to Moses,

> Give ear, O heavens, and I will speak;
> and let the earth hear the words of my mouth.
> May my teaching drop as the rain,
> my speech distil as the dew,
> as the gentle rain upon the tender grass,

and as showers upon the herb.
For I will proclaim the name of the Lord.
Ascribe greatness to our God!

Deuteronomy 32:1-3

SUGGESTIONS FOR STUDY AND DISCUSSION

New Testament use of Deuteronomy

Deuteronomy is so basic to a full understanding of the Gospels that it is not possible here to list all references. Here are a few:

The temptations of Jesus: Matthew 4:4, 7; cf. Deuteronomy 6:13

The call to repentance: Matthew 3:1; 4:17

Jesus' attitude to the Law: Matthew 5:17–end

The kingdom of God, the Fatherhood of God, are some of the concepts found in Deuteronomy; suggest others.

For discussion

1. Prophets are individuals. How are we to know they are hearing aright?

2. What do you see as the 'idols' of today's society? Are there any ways in which as individuals or as a God-fearing community we can help to lead the nation to God?

3. Is a 'holy community' possible, or should we aim only for holy individuals?

Conclusion:

What does the Pentateuch mean for us today?

HOPES FOR THE FUTURE

Men and women everywhere dream of a good time coming, when all shall be peace and justice. Some think of it as a Utopia on earth, some as a heavenly paradise. Some hope to achieve it by a particular ideology enforced by the government of the day, be it separate development, communism, or National Front. The Jewish priests expected it through right worship, while the Deuteronomists dreamt of a realm of justice and mercy, when man would so truly love his neighbour that he would leave grain in his field so that poor people could glean it. The child of 'God's steadfast love' would never 'sell the needy' for his own luxury, nor keep overnight a poor man's blanket as a pledge of debt. When there seemed no sign of any fulfilment of those ideals, there arose other hopes. Some looked for a messiah, a specially sent messenger of God to inaugurate his rule on earth, his kingdom, perhaps as ruler of the House of David, or one who would be heaven-sent, coming in clouds of glory.

Some such dream of a messiah had inspired the fight against Antiochus Epiphanes in the second century BC, and lay behind the writing of the book of Daniel, but in spite of much dedication, even these efforts came to nothing. After the fighting against Greek domination had ceased there was a period of relative calm, during which, in spite of internal struggles for power, those learned in the Law searched the Scriptures earnestly. They believed it was the expression of the will of God; could his people but follow it his kingdom would come. All agreed on the authority of the Torah, and all hoped for the coming of the kingdom of God, but there were even then many opinions about the way the Torah should be interpreted. These had tended in time to crystallize into opposing groups whose names are familiar to us from the New Testament.

WAYS OF INTERPRETING THE TORAH

Those from wealthier families who had prestige and political influence, the Sadducees, were prepared to compromise with their foreign overlords provided they could continue temple sacrifices. Their devotion to the Torah was such that they would accept neither the oral traditions that had grown up around it nor the ideas that were circulating at the time. They accepted the priestly view of history as found in the Torah (and described in chapter 8), thinking that the present epoch would end with the coming of the messiah. They hoped for the coming of God's kingdom through the observance of the priestly rules for worship. So long as the government allowed this to continue, the Sadducees were not prepared to fight against it. On the other hand were those who had rallied to the cause of Judas Maccabeus determined to remove any traces of Hellenism. They gradually separated into different groups, one of which, known as the Zealots, was prepared to continue fighting to establish the holy community. Another, the Pharisees, accepted the prophetic view that the kingdom of God would come only when men and women obeyed his will. Some of these, especially those living away from Jerusalem, were more flexible in their approach and were prepared to interpret the regulations in the light of existing circumstances. The efforts of all Pharisees were directed to personal piety. They explained the reason for laws that were now obsolete; they tried to apply other laws to each detail of everyday life. In their zeal to achieve this, they added extra regulations. These teachings, known as 'The Traditions of the Elders', were codified in the Mishnah, or Teaching, (c. AD200) and form the basis of the Talmud, an important source of comment on the Torah for Jews through the ages.

Yet other groups of those who had fought for Judaism returned to the desert, there to establish religious communities to await the coming of the Messiah. The Qumran community, whose buried treasures were discovered in 1947, was one of these. Their writings, known as the Dead Sea Scrolls, show reverence for both Torah and Prophets, and also an apocalyptic expectation of the coming of the Messiah. In preparation for the latter they drew up plans for a holy war, the war of the sons of light against the sons of darkness. Although their influence may be seen behind some of the New Testament writings their teaching differs in many ways from that of Jesus. At the time when the Holy Land was under Roman occupation there were thus several groups interpreting some of the many books which had been written during the preceding years. Yet whatever their differences, all groups were united in their reverence for the Torah.

When the Romans destroyed Jerusalem in AD70, it seemed that once again the very survival of the Jews was threatened, and study of the Scriptures again intensified. The Sadducees had ceased to have any influence after the destruction of the temple had made sacrifice impossible. The Zealots continued to pursue their aim of fighting for freedom. One of the Pharisees, a rabbi named Johannen ben Zakkai, who had escaped from the siege of Jerusalem started a school in Jamnia, on the coast. Here some of the ablest of the Jewish leaders joined him. It was as a result of their influence that the 'Canon' of Scripture was finally settled, some years after most of the books in the New Testament had been written.

UNDERSTANDING THE PENTATEUCH

For Jews today, the Pentateuch is still the prime revelation of the will of God, and for that reason alone is worth our study. For Christians there is yet another reason, that both John the Baptist and Jesus, who each begun his ministry with the call, 'Repent, for the kingdom of God is at hand,' were brought up to reverence it from their earliest childhood. We cannot understand the Gospels without some understanding of the Pentateuch. A scientific and literary study of it may help to solve some of its puzzles, but this is not 'understanding', as Robert Runcie reminded the Vacation Term of Biblical Studies in 1985. He drew attention to the derivation of the word, and of its German equivalent, *versehen*, 'to stand in front of', pointing out that each 'suggests a *posture* of "waiting upon", of being attentive, reverent, ready and eager to receive whatever may be told, disclosed or given. One might even call it an obedient posture—for the Latin root of the word "obey" means "to put oneself in a position to hear" '. This was the attitude of John the Baptist and of Jesus, as it is of many people today, both Jews and Christians. To quote John Keble, 'The personal word is everywhere in the written word.'

Even before we are able to read, we listen to stories. Story-telling has from ancient times been the chief means of conveying wisdom from one generation to another. In studying the Patriarchs we recognized three different types of story, saga, cult-legend and myth. 'Cult-legends' are those stories which have been recited in ceremonies surrounding a holy place, recounting something of its origin. 'Myth' in common parlance often means something that never happened, but this is neither the original nor the present theological meaning of the term. Even though the characters in the story may never have existed in real life, the tale about them is told in such a way as to illustrate a fundamental truth. The story of Adam and Eve is a myth; as the children said, it is true to life, a parable of what life is like. 'Saga' consists of tales which have collected about people who probably actually lived, although so long ago that their existence cannot be scientifically proved. This makes little difference to their value, since, like the stories of King Arthur, these sagas are the means of passing on information and ideals. Saga is always 'true to life'. We are today re-discovering the value of story-telling. Not only is it both pleasurable and memorable; it allows ideas to penetrate more deeply than a mere statement of fact can do. Do we have to take these stories literally, for example, the ass that spoke, the five hundred thousand men of military age who crossed the Red Sea? Are they like Dick Whittington's cat, and Cinderella's pumpkin? If instead of asking, 'Did they actually happen?' we ask rather, 'What truths do these stories convey to us?' we are putting ourselves in the right posture, 'standing under' in order to 'understand'.

One of the first things a child learns from the tales is that everything comes right in the end. God is in charge, and he is just. He punishes the bad and rewards the good. Children are not told about the less respectable characters! A grown woman reading a modern translation for the first time was so thrilled that she read Genesis straight through. Her comment was one of shocked surprise. 'They weren't very *good* people, were they?' Of course not, they were ordinary sinful, fallible human beings like all of us, a mixture of good and evil. However, the Bible is about men and women only in so far as they are related to God's purpose; their stories are strung together to reveal a more surprising story in which the chief 'actor' is God himself. Yet God was able to establish his purpose through those who 'heard' his voice, and obeyed. Like children, the Israelites learnt the majesty of God only as their horizons widened. Here is the incredible belief, that the Creator of all that is visible and invisible is active in the affairs of men and women. God is in charge of the world he has made. He is not the remote 'Prime Mover of the universe' of Aristotle, neither is he the utterly unknowable 'Supreme God' of Hindu mythology. He is far from being the arbitrary gods of Greek mythology who treat mankind as playthings for their own pleasure. The God of the Hebrews dwells in the midst of his people, 'a very present help in trouble'. Many young people, like Abraham, know God first as the One to whom they can speak in their hearts. This is the personal relationship promised to Abraham, and basic to the covenant. 'You shall be my people, and I will be your God.' Some never grow beyond it, so that he becomes, 'God in your pocket'! This truth of his close presence must be held in tension with the complementary belief of God's kingship. God is both immanent and transcendent. These beliefs cannot be scientifically established; they are not subject to rational proof. They are 'known' to those men and women who from biblical times to the present have lived by this faith.

The stories of Abraham and Moses show that God establishes his kingship, not as a dictator, but through the willing obedience of 'true to life', ordinary men and women. His purpose is seen to be the redemption of the world through the co-operation of men and women who hear and obey. The story of the exodus is the supreme myth; it is found throughout the history of Israel. This is the principle which underlies the Law. 'I am the Lord, your God who has brought you out of the land of Egypt, out of the house of bondage.' The Lord, the great I AM, has acted, and continues to act to set his people free, free to serve him without fear.

WHAT IS OUR REASONABLE SERVICE?

All this we may learn from the stories; what of the laws? Are we to serve him by keeping every detail of every law? If not, how do we decide? Who decides? Some of the regulations are manifestly impossible for us, and it is doubtful whether even the most orthodox Jews want to return to the practice of sacrifice. We have seen that the regulations have been modified and elaborated as men have seen the need of their own age. If we see them as paths to the kingdom of God and keep this goal firmly in our vision we need not be worried that we cannot keep the Law in its entirety. The basic principle remains constant—loyalty to a God who saves. The *Shema* reduces the Ten Commandments to one, a total love of God. This is the way Paul, who described himself as being a 'Pharisee of the Pharisees' came to understand it. In his letter to the Romans, he struggled with this very question of the position of the Law, which he reverenced as 'the Oracles of God'. He likened the Torah to the trusted slave who escorted a child to the master who would educate him. He was convinced that righteousness based on law could not succeed in keeping the law; all was based on the mercy of God. Only a life of faith, lived in the Spirit, could achieve the righteousness which is indeed the free gift of God (Romans 3:21; Galatians 3:23; Romans 9:16; etc.).

This is the way Jesus, in the tradition of the prophets, had interpreted the Law. Austin Farrer in a sermon to undergraduates said,

> Ask yourself, not, What did God permit? ... nor, How much does God exact? but, What did the Lord who gave each law desire from willing servants, not to say loyal sons? He commands you to love your neighbour, does He desire you to hate your enemy? He directs judges to award exact retribution if a case be brought to court. Does He desire that suits be brought, rather than injuries forgiven? He forbids adultery; what lusts does He approve? Honour the Sabbath by a holy rest, love your neighbour as yourself. But see, it is a Sabbath, you are a healer and your neighbour is in pain; what does the Lord who gave you these commands desire that you should do?

Abraham was not looking to any code of law when he ventured into the unknown at the call of God, neither was Moses struggling to observe a moral law. They heard, and they obeyed, and so the will of God was accomplished. The moral code which has been accepted in the West for centuries is given in the Decalogue. This is in the form of commandments issued by an overlord. *but Othen* The prophets realized that what was required was not total submission to a tyrant but response to a loving God. They learnt to think of his demands as always merciful, always working for man's salvation. The prophet of the exile who spoke of the sufferings of God's servant also said,

> Fear not, for I have redeemed you;
> I have called you by name, you are mine.
> When you pass through the waters,
> I will be with you;
> And through the rivers, they shall not overwhelm you.

> *Isaiah 43:1f.*

The *hesed* of the Lord, his faithfulness to the covenant promise, his steadfast love, is the overwhelming revelation of the Pentateuch. Again and again in the early stories J has shown us the gentle care of the Lord for sinning man and woman. P and J together tell of the fresh start after the great flood, with God's promise that he would never again destroy mankind. The story of the exodus and of the journeys in the wilderness reveal a patient and forbearing Creator redeeming situations which seemed humanly hopeless. This steadfast love is far beyond ordinary human love, but we have no other way in which to describe it.

> *Can a woman forget her sucking child*
> *that she have no compassion on the son of her womb?*
> *Even these may forget,*
> *yet I will not forget you.*
> *Behold I have graven you in the palms of my hands.*

> Isaiah 49:15f

Prophets, who like Abraham had listened to the voice of God, were confident alike of the kingship of God and of his forgiveness. Their faith was no facile dream; it had been tested through times of great hardship, even to death. During the exile, Deutero-Isaiah declared an oracle of the everlasting God, the great I AM,

> *Who created the heavens and stretched them out,*
> *who spread forth the earth and all that comes*
> *from it, who gives breath to the people upon it*
> *and spirit to those who walk in it;*
> *I am the Lord, I have called you in righteousness,*
> *I have taken you by the hand and kept you;*
> *I have given you as a covenant to the people,*
> *a light to the nations,*
> *to open the eyes that are blind.*

> Isaiah 42:5f

It was not alone for Israel's sake that the Lord would forgive, but that his steadfast love might be known to all men.

> It is not for your sake alone, O house of Israel that I am about to act, but for the sake of my holy name, which you have profaned among the nations to which you came... the nations will know that I am the Lord.
>
> *Ezekiel 36:22f.*

THE FULFILMENT OF DREAMS?

Jews meet on the Day of Atonement to acknowledge their failures and their sinfulness, and to renew their relationship with God. The ceremony begins with the blowing of the *shofar* the ram's horn, a solemn reminder of the ram in the thicket which Abraham saw when he had surrendered his only son in response to God's call. It is a dramatic recall to obedience. It is, however a reminder not only to each individual present, but to the congregation as a whole. Throughout the Pentateuch, individuals are called, not for their own salvation, but for the sake of others. Even the chosen people, the *ecclesia* are called on behalf of others; they are to be a royal priesthood. Here are two more truths which must be held in tension! At the beginning of the Passover Festival, Jews are reminded that 'it is incumbent for every person to say, "I personally was brought out of Egypt, and I celebrate this Passover because God saved *me*" '. The responsibility rests on each person, but not for themselves alone. On the first night of the feast, Rabbi Albert Friedland wrote, 'the ten plagues are recited, and a drop of wine is removed from the ritual cup of joy with the mention of each plague, as a sign of grief; how can one fully rejoice when others suffer?' On the last day of the feast, when the Song of the Sea is sung, the rabbis add this commentary:

> When the children of Israel stood at the shore of the sea and sang, 'Who is like unto Thee, O Lord?' the heavenly choirs of angels joined in that song. God rebuked them sharply, and they stopped in amazement. 'Why should we not sing?' they asked, 'Look! Your children have escaped across the sea, and they praise you for saving them!' 'That is true', said God. 'My children of Israel now rejoice in their freedom. But are not the Egyptians my children as well? And are they not drowning in the sea? It is a time of grief as well as of rejoicing.'

Rabbi Albert Friedland wrote that on a recent visit to Israel he found much compassion and understanding for the sufferings of the Palestinians, with desperate efforts to find a political solution—in spite of the militancy and hatred which surrounds Israel on all sides. There is tension within Israel too. Fairly recently the Jewish Professor of Greek Patrology at the Hebrew University—do you find this a surprising study for a Hebrew?—began a discussion by saying, 'The Jewish concept of love is expressed in the conquest of Jericho. Joshua destroyed the people of Jericho in the name of God, because he loved his own people ... Christian love is the seemingly impossible love. Something amazing to behold. It is the love of the crucified who says, "Father, forgive them, for they know not what they do." ' This statement caused a violent division among his hearers. There were some who felt they should fight, like Joshua, for the purity of God's elect. The prophets had visions of a time when a covenant of peace would unite all of the warring factions—Egypt and Israel, Ishmael and Jacob. These dreams await fulfilment! All Jews worship the one God whom the Pentateuch reveals as steadfast love; each thinks his own interpretation the only one. The dreams of all await fulfilment.

CHRISTIAN UNDERSTANDING

Christians believe that in Jesus they have seen the true interpretation. His understanding of the Law was similar to Abraham's hearing and obeying the 'voice of God'. During the Roman occupation when expectation of a messiah was running high, some liberal thinkers felt the laws should be brought up to date. Others felt this process would lead to secularization. Jesus seemed to be saying that these difficulties would disappear if people regarded the book of the Law rightly, as the expression of the mind of God for his children. He went behind the written law to seek for the will of God. This is the way he lived, showing integrity and compassion in all his words and deeds. He was often accused of breaking the Law by those who tried to keep its letter, but he lived in complete obedience as a son to a loving Father. Those who tried to follow his way found a new sense of community. Eventually the Jewish community repudiated them. Those who were trying to follow the way of Jesus acclaimed him as Messiah, and thought of themselves as the people of the new covenant, the new Israel. They interpreted his death and resurrection as a new exodus. Jesus had revealed to them the Word of God. He had so lived and died that they saw in him the steadfast love of God. As the Gospel of Saint John puts it, 'The Word was

hesed

made flesh and dwelt among us.' It is granted to each generation through the fulness of God's creative love, to find in the Bible, and in the incarnate Word just what is needed for its own spirit.

Frequently, we read in the Gospels, 'He that has ears to hear, let him hear.' This is the attitude to which Jews are recalled by the *shofar*. Christians learn it through the stories which surround the mystery of the birth of Jesus. Sentences from these tales form the main body of the *Angelus*, which has been repeated down the ages. Like the *shofar* it is a reminder of the love of God, and a call for human obedience. It consists of the angel's words to Mary, and those of Elizabeth, coupled with a request for Mary's prayer. It is this request that many people find unacceptable, but the general theme of the whole is inherent in the Pentateuch. God initiates, his child obeys, and so his will is accomplished.

The angel of the Lord appeared to Mary.
And Mary said, 'Behold the handmaid of the Lord'.
And the Word was made flesh, and dwelt among us.

Index

+shofar p124